An Aviator's Field Guide to the
Seaplane Rating

An Aviator's Field Guide to the
Seaplane Rating

Knowledge and practical skills training to add a seaplane rating to your pilot certificate

William O. Young

AVIATION SUPPLIES & ACADEMICS, INC.
NEWCASTLE, WASHINGTON

An Aviator's Field Guide to the Seaplane Rating
Knowledge and practical skills training to add a seaplane rating to your pilot certificate
by William O. Young

Aviation Supplies & Academics, Inc.
7005 132nd Place SE
Newcastle, Washington 98059
asa@asa2fly.com | 425-235-1500 | asa2fly.com

Copyright © 2025 Aviation Supplies & Academics, Inc.

See the Reader Resources at **asa2fly.com/seaplane** for additional information and updates relating to this book.

All Rights Reserved. No part of this publication may be reproduced, stored in a retrieval system, or transmitted in any form or by any means without the prior written permission of the copyright holder. No part of this publication may be used in any manner for the purpose of training artificial intelligence systems or technologies. While every precaution has been taken in the preparation of this book, the publisher and William O. Young assume no responsibility for damages resulting from the use of the information contained herein.

None of the material in this book supersedes any operational documents or procedures issued by the Federal Aviation Administration, aircraft and avionics manufacturers, flight schools, or the operators of aircraft.

ASA-SEAPLANE
ISBN 978-1-64425-389-2

Additional formats available:
eBook EPUB   ISBN 978-1-64425-390-8
eBook PDF   ISBN 978-1-64425-391-5

Printed in the United States of America.
2029   2028   2027   2026   2025   9   8   7   6   5   4   3   2   1

Cover photo: iStock.com/juvat092.

Library of Congress Cataloging-in-Publication Data
Names: Young, William O., 1956- author.
Title: An aviator's field guide to the seaplane rating : knowledge and practical skills training to add a seaplane rating to your pilot certificate / William O. Young.
Description: Newcastle, Washington : Aviation Supplies & Academics, Inc., [2025] | Includes index.
Identifiers: LCCN 2024040881 (print) | ISBN 9781644253892 (trade paperback) | ISBN 9781644253908 (epub) | ISBN 9781644253915 (pdf)
Subjects: LCSH: Seaplanes—Piloting. | Seaplanes—Piloting—Handbooks, manuals, etc. | Seaplanes—Piloting—Examinations—Study guides.
Classification: LCC TL711.S43 Y68 2025 (print) | LCC TL711.S43 (ebook) | DDC 629.132/52—dc23/eng/20241108
LC record available at https://lccn.loc.gov/2024040881
LC ebook record available at https://lccn.loc.gov/2024040882

Contents

Acknowledgments ix

PREFACE: For Seaplane Instructors xi
   How to Use This Book xi
   A Seaplane Instructor's Guide to the Airman Certification
      Standards (ACS) xiv
   Pre-Checkride Paperwork xvii

Introduction: For Students xix
   How to Use This Book xx

1 Arriving Prepared for ASES Training 1

2 ASES Syllabus 5
   Ground Lesson 1: Seaplane Basics 6
   Ground Lesson 2: Getting to Know Your
      Training Aircraft 8
   Ground Lesson 3: Preflight through Takeoff 10
   Ground Lesson 4: Water Landings 12
   Ground Lesson 5: Beaching, Docking, Emergency
      Procedures, and Odds and Ends 14
   Flight Lesson 1: Handling the Aircraft in the Air and on
      the Water 16
   Flight Lesson 2: Water Takeoffs and Landings—Normal 18
   Flight Lesson 3: Water Takeoffs and Landings—the
      Other Kinds 20
   Flight Lesson 4: Beaching, Docking, Emergency
      Procedures, and Review 21

v

3 Seabird 1850/1850A Data 23

Specifications and Limitations 24

Performance 25

Performance Data 25

Seabird 1850 Takeoff and Landing Data 26

Seabird 1850A Takeoff and Landing Data—Water 28

Seabird 1850A Takeoff and Landing Data—Land 30

4 Checklists: Normal and Emergency 33

Normal Procedures 33

Preflight 33

Before Starting Engine 36

Starting Engine 37

Before Takeoff 38

Takeoff 39

Normal Climb 40

Cruise 40

Descent 41

Before Landing 41

Landing 42

After Landing 43

After Operating In Water 44

Selected Emergency Procedures 45

Engine Failure 45

Power-off Landing 46

Landing Gear Malfunctions 46

Electrical System Malfunctions 48

5 Study Guide 49

The Briefest Seaplane History Lesson Ever 49

Seaplane Basics 50

Transitioning to Water Flying: What to Expect 51

Are We Flying, or Are We Boating? 54

Reading the Water Surface 61

Clues to Wind Speed 61

Clues to Wind Direction 63

Assessing the Landing Area 63

Preflight Procedures 64

Maneuvering on the Water ... 67
   Taxiing ... 67
   Turning on the Water ... 70
   A Note on Porpoising ... 71
   Taxiing Downwind ... 72
   J-Turn for Takeoff in Confined Area ... 72
   Sailing ... 73
Water Takeoffs ... 74
   Normal Water Takeoff ... 75
   Crosswind Water Takeoff ... 76
   Glassy Water Takeoff ... 77
   Rough Water Takeoff ... 78
   Confined Area Water Takeoff ... 80
   After Takeoff ... 81
Water Landings ... 82
   Preparing for Water Landing ... 82
   Normal Water Landing ... 88
   Crosswind Water Landing ... 88
   Glassy Water Landing ... 90
   Rough Water Landing ... 92
   Confined Area Water Landing ... 94
   Power-Off Emergency Landing ... 95
Beaching ... 96
Docking ... 97
Runway Operations in an Amphibious Seaplane ... 100
   Taxiing ... 100
   Takeoff ... 101
   Landing ... 103

6 Oral Exam Preparation Questions ... **105**
Questions ... 106
Answers ... 121

7 Preparing for the Practical Test ... **139**

**8 Congratulations—You Earned Your Seaplane Rating!
Now What?** ... **143**

Contents *vii*

Appendix A: More Than You May Want to Know About the ACS **149**

Appendix B: A Sampling of Seaplane Checklist Mnemonics **155**

Appendix C: More on Winds and Currents **163**

Index **173**

About the Author **177**

Acknowledgments

Nothing beats teaching for exposing the gaps in one's knowledge—the things you thought you knew until you tried to explain them to someone else. I am grateful to each of the pilots who have allowed me to be their seaplane instructor, but especially to Jimmy Foecking, who was a willing guinea pig as my very first seaplane student. Much of what is in this book was first tried out on Jimmy.

But before subjecting anyone to my seaplane instruction, I needed to gain enough experience to feel I had something worth passing along to students. For this there was no substitute for owning a seaplane and flying it a lot, and I am fortunate to have owned an amazingly capable and versatile aircraft, a Cessna 185 amphib. Here again I am indebted to Jimmy Foecking, who in addition to being my first seaplane student is also the A&P/IA who kept my aircraft flying. The late J. J. Frey gave generously of his time and expertise in teaching Jimmy and me how to maintain my Edo floats. My father, an engineer, designed and built equipment for my aircraft that greatly facilitated towing and maintenance of amphibious floatplanes.

While I have learned much from my experience (including mistakes) as a seaplane owner and pilot, and from my seaplane students' questions, the foundation for all of this was laid by my own seaplane instructors. The late Rich Hensch of Florida Seaplanes, Inc., provided my ASES training in a straight-float Maule M-7 and offered training materials that inspired me to produce a comprehensive training manual for my students. Lyle Panepinto of Southern Seaplane, Inc., taught me how to fly my 185 amphib and, through Southern Seaplane's outstanding Seaplane Safety Institute course, greatly broadened and deepened my seaplane knowledge and experience, and prepared me well to learn more on my own in the 185. And I was the first multi-engine seaplane student (in an Aircam) of Jeff Ward at WaterWings, LLC, whose owner, Charles Welden, has created a seaplane pilot's paradise in Alabama. I am grateful to all of these instructors for helping me in the ongoing process of becoming a competent and safe seaplane pilot and instructor, and for making it possible for me to experience the beauty and fun of flying seaplanes.

Chris Mackey clarified several Airman Certification Standards (ACS) questions for me. I am grateful to him and to all of my instructors for their help, but any errors that remain in the book are mine alone.

Preface:
For Seaplane Instructors

How to Use This Book

While you may occasionally have a student who wants to earn a Private or Commercial Pilot Certificate from start to finish in a seaplane, the vast majority of pilots who get a seaplane rating do it as an add-on to an existing Private or Commercial Pilot Certificate. This book is not a comprehensive guide to private or commercial pilot training. Instead, it is meant for pilots who currently hold a Private or Commercial Pilot Certificate with an Airplane Single-Engine Land (ASEL) and/or Airplane Multi-Engine Land (AMEL) rating and who are training for an Airplane Single-Engine Sea (ASES) add-on to their existing pilot certificate. (As explained below, pilots who currently hold an Airline Transport Pilot [ATP] certificate will be getting a commercial, not ATP, ASES add-on.)

Several excellent seaplane books are already available. For example, Burke Mees's *Notes of a Seaplane Instructor* significantly shortened my learning curve as an instructor and taught me several nuances that I didn't pick up in my ASES training. The late J. J. Frey's *How to Fly Floats* has made me a better seaplane pilot. And there are seaplane books that are encyclopedic in their scope and depth, such as Dale DeRemer's *Seaplane Pilot*, to which I refer often when I need more detail on various seaplane topics. I recommend all of these to you and to your students as they continue their seaplane education.

xi

But I am not aware of an existing book that is intended as a concise hands-on training manual for the ASES rating, designed for students to use actively, before and during their training, as opposed to being used only as a reference book to pull off the shelf and look things up in. And I am not aware of another seaplane training guide in which the curriculum and oral examination prep questions are deliberately ACS-directed, so that students and instructors can be sure their training is consistent with the latest ACS requirements.

While there is far more to learn about flying floats than is contained in this book, it does include what the student needs—not much more, but not less—to earn the Airplane Single-Engine Sea (ASES) rating with confidence, and to begin the process of becoming a competent and safe seaplane pilot. This manual is short enough that your students can realistically read and digest it *before* and during their seaplane training, yet thorough enough to help you prepare them well for the ASES practical test.

You could create your own training manual for your own students in your own aircraft, as I did, but this book may save you the trouble (or may at least give you ideas for your own manual!).

I do feel strongly that it's better for both the student and the instructor when the student arrives prepared for training, so I would ask you to consider recommending that your students who will be using this book get started on it *before* they come to you for training. (See my comments in the Introduction, which like the remainder of the book is addressed to students, regarding what to read carefully, what to skim, and what to skip until they arrive to train with you.) There are other resources that I think are also helpful in preparing students for their training with you; I have listed these in Chapter 1, Arriving Prepared for Seaplane Training. You will no doubt have recommendations to add to mine.

I think veteran seaplane instructors and novice seaplane instructors will use this book differently. Veteran seaplane instructors will already have settled on a ground and flight training curriculum that works for them and for their students, so for them the curriculum in this book may be of little use.

But I hope instructors who are new to seaplane instruction will find that the curriculum gives them a useful starting point

xii **Preface:** For Seaplane Instructors

for developing their own curriculum. Perhaps they will use the curriculum in this book as is with their first few students, and then modify it as they see fit based on their growing experience.

And new seaplane instructors may benefit more than veteran instructors from this book's exposition of ACS requirements (more details below and in Appendix A), IACRA guidance, and summary of the specific logbook endorsements required before the ASES practical test.

For all instructors, this book provides your students with a place to record data specific to your aircraft as well as your specific preferences regarding how to fly your training aircraft. As mentioned later in the comments addressed to students, the book is meant to be written in.

I hope you will see that a safety mindset is a theme of the book. And throughout, especially in the oral exam preparation questions (Chapter 6), I have tried to incorporate scenario-based training and to emphasize the use of checklists and of your preferred flows.

And finally, of interest (I hope) to all instructors, I have directly addressed the most recent Airman Certification Standards (ACS) in this book. Your primary objective is to train competent and safe seaplane pilots, and I believe this book will help you do that. But there's no getting around the fact that the examiner who gives your student the practical test will be conducting the oral examination and flight test according to ACS standards, and your seaplane student will be responsible for specific ACS tasks. The tasks required depend on whether the student currently holds a Private or Commercial Pilot Certificate, and on whether the student holds a Multi-Engine Rating. It is a bit of a maze to figure out which ACS tasks ASES add-on candidates will be responsible for on the ASES checkride—and there have been changes in the tasks required in the most recent editions of the Private and Commercial ACSs— but I have sorted that out in the section below titled "A Seaplane Instructor's Guide to the Airman Certification Standards" and in Appendix A.

In Chapter 6, Oral Exam Preparation Questions, each ACS task required of any candidate for ASES add-on is addressed by at least one question, and many tasks are addressed by several questions.

Preface: For Seaplane Instructors *xiii*

The task(s) addressed by each question are shown. Similarly, in the curriculum for ground and flight training in Chapter 2, ASES Syllabus, I have noted which ACS tasks are addressed in each lesson.

My goal here is to give you and your students confidence that your training will address all ACS tasks they will be responsible for on the checkride.

In summary, I hope this book will help both you and your students make the most of their ASES training and will inspire them to continue their education as competent and safe seaplane pilots.

A Seaplane Instructor's Guide to the Airman Certification Standards (ACS)

Seaplane training is fun for both students and instructors, and the whole atmosphere of seaplane training is more casual than that of most other flight training. But while a written test is not required, getting the ASES rating does require a practical test (oral exam and flight test) with an FAA Designated Pilot Examiner (DPE), just like any other FAA certificate or rating, and that is something students and instructors should never take lightly.

Just as with practical tests for other certificates and ratings, examiners for the ASES rating are required to assess whether candidates meet the established standards for the relevant tasks detailed in the Airman Certification Standards (ACS). For each of about a dozen "areas of operation," the ACS specifies the tasks that candidates must demonstrate mastery of. Each task includes the knowledge elements the candidate must know, the risk management issues the candidate must understand, and the skills the candidate must demonstrate on the flight test.

There is no separate ACS for the ASES add-on. Instead, the ASES add-on requirements are found in a grid in Appendix 1 of the *Private Pilot for Airplane Category Airman Certification Standards* (FAA-S-ACS-6C) and the *Commercial Pilot for Airplane Category Airman Certification Standards* (FAA-S-ACS-7B).

There is no grid for ASES add-on in the Airline Transport Pilot (ATP) ACS, meaning that there is no such thing as an ASES add-on for an ATP certificate. A pilot can obtain an ASES ATP certificate,

xiv **Preface:** For Seaplane Instructors

but only by doing a full ATP checkride in a single-engine seaplane—if the pilot can find a designated seaplane ATP examiner, of which there are very few. So for practical purposes, if a pilot who currently holds a land ATP certificate comes to you for ASES training, they will be getting a commercial ASES add-on, not an ATP ASES certificate, and they will be held to Commercial ACS standards on the checkride.

In Appendix A of this book, I present the Private and Commercial ASES add-on grids together for comparison, and I go into great detail about the implications. For further details regarding these grids, including an explanation of the ASES add-on requirements for those few private and commercial pilots who hold AMEL ratings without ASEL, see Appendix A.

But the remainder of this section pertains to the vast majority of ASES add-on candidates, namely private or commercial pilots who hold at least an ASEL rating, with or without AMEL.

Let's skip to the bottom line: What ACS tasks are all private and commercial ASES add-on candidates (again, assuming they hold at least ASEL) responsible for on the checkride?

- Performance and Limitations
- Operation of Systems
- Water and Seaplane Characteristics, Seaplane Bases, Maritime Rules, and Aids to Marine Navigation
- Human Factors
- Preflight Assessment
- Flight Deck Management
- Taxiing and Sailing
- Before Takeoff Check
- Traffic Patterns
- Normal Takeoff and Climb
- Normal Approach and Landing
- Confined Area Takeoff and Maximum Performance Climb
- Confined Area Approach and Landing

Preface: For Seaplane Instructors *xv*

- Glassy Water Takeoff and Climb
- Glassy Water Approach and Landing
- Rough Water Takeoff and Climb
- Rough Water Approach and Landing
- Seaplane Post-Landing Procedures

In addition, again assuming they currently hold at least a ASEL rating, private ASES add-on candidates (but not commercial ASES add-on candidates) will be responsible for the following tasks:

- Emergency Descent
- Emergency Approach and Landing (Simulated)

Each of these required ACS tasks has associated knowledge, risk management, and skill elements that are spelled out explicitly in the ACS. On the practical test, for each task, the examiner is required to test at least one knowledge element, at least one risk management element, and all skill elements.

And a final note regarding the examiner's latitude on the checkride: The tasks named in the add-on grids are the required tasks. Since your student already holds a Private or Commercial Pilot Certificate, the examiner is within their rights to test your student on anything in the respective (i.e., private or commercial) ACS. In my experience, examiners seldom test ASES add-on candidates on ACS tasks other than the required ones—but they can.

Here's the point of all this. The ACS tells you what your student will be responsible for knowing and/or demonstrating on the practical test, so it is your job to make sure that you cover (at least) all of the required tasks in the course of your training. This manual is intended to help you do that.

xvi **Preface:** For Seaplane Instructors

Pre-Checkride Paperwork

You may have covered all the ACS bases in your training, and your student may be impeccably prepared, but the examiner still can't even begin the practical test, much less issue the rating, if your endorsements in the student's logbook are not in order.

All ASES candidates will need the following endorsements:

- 14 CFR §61.31(d)(2)—To act as PIC in this seaplane (a class for which the student is not yet rated).

- 14 CFR §61.63(c)—Endorsement for additional class rating (Sea).

- 14 CFR §61.39(a)(6)—Your statement that the candidate has received the required training from you and is prepared for the practical test.

In addition, depending on the particulars of the aircraft you're using and on whether the candidate already has these endorsements, the candidate may need the following:

- 14 CFR §61.31(e)—Complex endorsement.

- 14 CFR §61.31(f)—High-performance airplane endorsement.

Sample wording for these endorsements can be found in the latest version of FAA Advisory Circular (AC) 61-65, *Certification: Pilots and Flight and Ground Instructors*, Appendix A.

And then there's IACRA, the FAA's Integrated Airman Certification and Rating Application system.

Remember to advise your student to submit their own IACRA application by the day *before* the checkride, so you both have time to address any questions or problems the student may have with the application. Note: the IACRA Help Desk really works. It's available 24 hours a day, and when you call 1-844-FAA-MYIT (322-6948), you will reach an actual person who is familiar with IACRA. I have always found those who staff the help desk to be helpful.

After the student has successfully submitted their IACRA application (the day before the checkride, so neither of you has to worry about IACRA-related issues on the day of the checkride),

Preface: For Seaplane Instructors *xvii*

you need to log onto IACRA with your own FAA tracking number (FTN) in order to endorse the candidate's IACRA application as the Recommending Instructor. To do that, you'll need your student's FTN number.

The process for endorsing the student's IACRA application is described in Section 8: Recommending Instructor Process in the FAA IACRA User Guide available online at iacratraining.faa.gov.

Introduction:
For Students

A former airline pilot who has flown professionally for more than 30 years came to me for Airplane Single-Engine Sea (ASES) add-on training because he was considering buying a seaplane. Neither of us was surprised that he excelled in his seaplane training and had no difficulty whatsoever with the checkride. After the checkride, he told me, "I've got 14,000 hours, I've been a 747 captain, I've owned an airline, I've done this, I've done that—but *this* is the coolest thing I've done in aviation!"

By contrast, I had maybe 500 hours, all in piston singles, when I got my ASES rating. But my reaction at the time was exactly the same as his, and over the years I've found that this reaction is the rule, not the exception, among new seaplane pilots, regardless of what kind of flying they've done before—and I've also found that this feeling doesn't fade away. Before I had my seaplane rating, I had the opportunity to ride as a passenger on a Kenmore Air turbine de Havilland DHC-3 Otter flight from Roche Harbor in the San Juan Islands to Seattle's Lake Union. As we were boarding, the single pilot said (too quietly, I thought, because I almost missed it) that someone could sit in the right seat if they wanted to. I was at the back of the line of passengers waiting to board, and I may or may not have knocked women and children in the water as I sprinted for the front and jumped in the right seat. During our short but spectacularly beautiful flight I asked the grey-haired pilot, who was about to retire, what kind of flying he had done before. He thought for a while, and

xix

finally replied, "You know, I don't really remember. I came here when I was 18 to do this for a summer, and I just never saw a reason to do anything else." I understood completely.

There is something *liberating* about flying floats. Much of our "regular" flying is regimented and structured, and most of the time it really needs to be that way for safety. But in a seaplane, in addition to the fact that it's usually beautiful just to be on and above the water, you make many of your own rules. It's you, not an air traffic controller, who decides where and in what direction you're going to take off and land—and you may be the first person ever to land a seaplane where you're landing. You, and no one else, must find out whether there's a power line in your approach or departure path. There is almost never an ATIS or AWOS where you will be operating, so you must essentially build your own ATIS based on your observation of the water surface and surroundings. When flying seaplanes, you spend most of your time at much lower altitudes than when flying land planes, and you sometimes may ask yourself, as you're skimming over treetops on approach to a landing on a lake, "Do we really get to do this?" (We do.) And when operating seaplanes, you must develop (just like a sailor) a constant awareness of, and ability to assess, the speed and direction of the wind, both while flying and while taxiing on the water. And in the end maybe that is the essence of flying floats: Operating a seaplane safely requires you to be more self-reliant, and more observant of and connected to your environment, than any other form of fixed-wing flying.

So this is the world you're about to enter, and I'm excited for you. The goal of this book is to help you get the most out of your seaplane training, and to help you on your way to becoming a competent and safe seaplane pilot.

How to Use This Book

Think of this book as a training manual, not as a textbook. It is not meant to sit on the shelf but instead to be read, referred to, and written in before and throughout your seaplane training.

And I did say "before." As a student, I like to be as prepared as I can be before starting training, and as a teacher, I am much more effective when the student shows up prepared. Help yourself and your instructor by skimming the entire book, but *carefully read the entire Study Guide* (Chapter 5), and skim the oral examination preparation questions (Chapter 6) and the lesson plans (Chapter 2), beginning a couple of weeks before you begin your training.

And note also that this book is intended to be used in *addition to,* **not** *instead of,* the other resources listed in Chapter 1, Arriving Prepared for ASES Training, as well as anything else your instructor asked you to read beforehand.

Note: *Do not* try to remember anything about the lesson plans, because your instructor will likely do things differently. Use them as a general guide to how things might go, but by all means, once you begin training, go only by your instructor's plan. (*Please* don't tell your instructor, "But it says right here that in Lesson 2 we should be doing such and such today.")

And *do not* try to learn any of the specifications, limitations, performance data, checklists, systems, or profiles (power settings, pitch attitudes, flap settings, and airspeeds for various phases of flight) for the Seabird (my fictitious seaplane introduced in Chapter 3 and used as an example in this book). Think of the information I have provided for the Seabird as a template for the things you will need to know about your training aircraft. In most cases, I have provided space for you to write the data for your training aircraft on the same page where the Seabird data are given.

Note that some procedures, checklists, and important safety considerations are specific to flying amphibious seaplanes. In this book, content that pertains only to amphib seaplanes is identified with an "Amphib" bracket in the margin, as shown here. These sections should be ignored by pilots of straight-float seaplanes.

Most floatplanes are flown similarly, so what your instructor tells you is likely going to be very similar to the procedures described in this book for the Seabird. But if your instructor

Introduction: For Students   *xxi*

teaches a procedure differently than described in this book for the Seabird, ***do it the way your instructor teaches it***. Your instructor will have found what works best for them (and for you) in that particular aircraft, and in that particular location, so do it their way. It won't differ drastically from what is in this book, but where there are differences, do it your instructor's way—and make notes on the pertinent page of the book regarding how they want it done.

So this book is meant to be written in. And since it will be with you as you train, and not back in the hotel room, it wouldn't surprise me if it got a little wet at times or if its pages got a little grease on them. And because it will be filled with your notes about your specific training aircraft and your instructor's preferences, once you get done with it, it will be of use only to someone training in the same aircraft and with the same instructor—but even they may not want it, because it's going to be so beat up. So keep it—and *then* it can go on the shelf, ready for you to review before your next seaplane flying opportunity.

xxii **Introduction: For Students**

Chapter 1
Arriving Prepared for ASES Training

You are about to experience the beauty, excitement, and fun of flying floats. It's an experience you'll never forget.

This will be the most fun flying you've ever done, but you do need to be aware that your seaplane training is a concentrated course, intended to be completed in two or three days. Your flight test will likely be scheduled with an FAA Designated Pilot Examiner (DPE) before you start your training. In order for you to learn what you need to know in such a short time, it is essential (in my opinion) that you do some studying before you begin your training. Training for your seaplane rating without advance preparation can be done, but it will take longer and will be considerably more expensive. And even with advance preparation, you can expect to be doing a fair amount of studying when you're not flying during the course itself.

So help your instructor, and yourself, by coming prepared. Before your training begins, *at least* complete the following:

- Study any materials/resources your instructor has asked you to read beforehand.

- Read the Study Guide (Chapter 5) and skim the Oral Exam Preparation Questions (Chapter 6) in this book. Your instructor will *not* expect you to know all of this before you start your training, but it is reasonable for them to expect that during your training you will be hearing at least some of what is being taught for the second time, not the first.

- Skim the Syllabus (Chapter 2) in this book to get an overview of a typical sequence of lessons, keeping in mind that your instructor may well have their own set curriculum. The curriculum in this book will at least give you an idea of what you'll be doing during your training, though perhaps in a different sequence.

Other useful resources to consider looking at in advance:

- FAA's *Seaplane, Skiplane, and Float/Ski Equipped Helicopter Operations Handbook* (FAA-H-8083-23), Chapters 1–6 and the glossary. This is to seaplane flying what the FAA's *Airplane Flying Handbook* is to regular flying. Because it is what the FAA has to say about seaplane flying, it's worth your time to be aware of its content. You may find this useful as a reference during and after the course. It is available as a PDF for free at www.faa.gov.

- YouTube video *Flying Floats* (about 20 minutes long), produced by the FAA in 1973 but still useful.[1]

And while I don't think you need to spend more money than you already have to prepare for your ASES training, be aware that there are seaplane courses available, including the following:

- The video course *So You Want To Fly Seaplanes* ($39.99 at Sporty's Pilot Shop).
- Gleim Seaplane Add-On Rating Course ($44.95 at various aviation supplies retailers).

What you will likely be asked to bring:

- Shorts (quick drying), soft rubber-soled shoes that you can get wet, sunglasses, hat
- Pilot certificate
- Current medical certificate
- Photo ID (driver's license is OK)

---

[1] "Flying Floats 1973 Vintage FAA Aviation Training Film," posted July 31, 2009, by AIRBOYD, YouTube video, 19:12, https://youtu.be/0Gk2itUOEpc.

- Logbook
- Payment for examiner's fee, payable on the day of the checkride
- Full course fee (or balance, if you have already made a deposit)

(iStock.com/edb3_16)

Chapter 2
ASES Syllabus

Below is a suggested schedule for completing the lessons provided on the following pages.

Day	Lesson	Topic	Duration (hours)	Completed
1	Ground 1	Seaplane basics	1.0	
1	Ground 2	Getting to know your training aircraft	1.0	
1	Ground 3	Preflight through takeoff	1.0	
1	Ground 4	Water landings	1.0	
1	Flight 1	Handling the aircraft in the air and on the water	1.5	
1	Flight 2	Water takeoffs and landings—normal	1.5	
2	Ground 5	Beaching, docking, emergency procedures, and odds and ends	1.0–1.5	
2	Flight 3	Water takeoffs and landings—the other kinds	1.5	
2 or 3	Flight 4	Beaching, docking, emergency procedures, and review	1.5	
2 or 3	Checkride			

Ground Lesson 1: Seaplane Basics

ACS Tasks Addressed:
Private: PA.I.I
Commercial: CA.I.I

Related Oral Exam Prep Questions:
See Chapter 6, questions 3, 12–16, 18–28.

Objectives:

- To explain the differences between seaplanes and land planes.
- To introduce the additional (and unfamiliar) factors that seaplane pilots must consider, including boating terminology and rules.

Resources:

- FAA-H-8083-23, Chapters 1, 2, and 5
- Chapter 5: Study Guide sections:
  - Seaplane Basics
  - Transitioning to Water Flying
  - Are We Flying, or Are We Boating?
  - Reading the Water Surface
  - Assessing the Landing Area
- Chapter 6: Oral Exam Preparation Questions (question numbers listed above) and answers
- *Flying Floats* video (optional; see Chapter 1)

1.0 hour

Content:

- Types of seaplanes
  - floatplane (straight/amphib) versus flying boat
- Transition to water flying—what to expect
- Are we flying, or are we boating?
- Clues to wind speed/direction
- Assessing the landing area

Completion Standards:

The student will understand:

- The types of seaplanes that exist
- The differences in flying characteristics of seaplanes and land planes
- The wind-related and water-related factors that must be considered in operating a seaplane
- Boating rules that apply to seaplane pilots

(iStock.com/ksteffens)

Ground Lesson 2:
Getting to Know Your Training Aircraft

ACS Tasks Addressed:
Private: PA.I.F, G; PA.IX.C
Commercial: CA.I.F, G; CA.IX.C

Related Oral Exam Prep Questions:
See Chapter 6, questions 1, 2, 4, 6–10, 35, 36.

Objectives:

- To familiarize the student with the specific aircraft that will be used for training.

Resources:

- Your training aircraft's airplane flight manual (AFM)/pilot's operating handbook (POH) and float supplement
- Your training aircraft's checklists (normal and emergency procedures)
- Chapter 6: Oral Exam Preparation Questions (question numbers listed above) and answers

1.0 hour

Content:

- Your training aircraft's specifications and limitations, including key airspeeds
- Your training aircraft's float details
- Your training aircraft's systems
- Your training aircraft's performance
- Your training aircraft's weight and balance data
- Your training aircraft's checklists (normal and emergency procedures) and "flows" (such as GUMPFARTS)

Completion Standards:

The student will become familiar with the training aircraft, to include:

- Specifications
- Limitations
- Float operation
- Systems
- Performance
- Weight and balance
- Checklists/flows

(iStock.com/WoodyUpstate)

Ground Lesson 3:
Preflight through Takeoff

ACS Tasks Addressed:
Private: PA.II.A, B, E, F; PA.IV.A, G, I, K
Commercial: CA.II.A, B, E, F; CA.IV.A, G, I, K

Related Oral Exam Prep Questions:
See Chapter 6, questions 29–34, 37–44, 46, 47, 50, 53, 54.

Objectives:

- To explain the steps that must be taken before flight and in preparation for takeoff in a seaplane.
- To encourage the habit of proper checklist usage.

Resources:

- FAA-H-8083-23, Chapter 4
- Chapter 5: Study Guide sections:
    - Preflight Procedures
    - Maneuvering on the Water
    - Water Takeoffs
- Chapter 6: Oral Exam Preparation Questions (question numbers listed above) and answers

1.0 hour

Content:

- Preflight procedures
- Checklist usage
- Maneuvering on the water
  - Idle taxi
  - Step taxi including turns
  - Plow taxi turns
  - Sailing
- Water takeoffs
  - Normal
  - Crosswind
  - Rough water
  - Glassy water
  - Confined area

Completion Standards:

The student will understand:

- The information that must be gathered before a seaplane flight
- Preflight inspection of a seaplane
- The pros and cons of idle taxiing, step taxiing, and plow taxi turns in various situations
- How (and when) to sail a seaplane
- How to perform normal, crosswind, rough water, glassy water, and confined area takeoffs

(iStock.com/jonathansloane)

Chapter 2—ASES Syllabus **11**

Ground Lesson 4: Water Landings

ACS Tasks Addressed:
Private: PA.III.B; PA.IV.B, H, J, L; PA.IV.M*
Commercial: CA.III.B; CA.IV.B, H, J, L

Related Oral Exam Prep Questions:
See Chapter 6, questions 11, 45, 49, 51, 52, 55, 56.

Objectives:
- To explain how to make all types of non-emergency water landings in a seaplane.
- To explain how to make a forward slip to a landing* in a seaplane.
- To encourage the habit of checklist usage.

Resources:
- FAA-H-8083-23, Chapter 5
- Chapter 5: Study Guide sections:
  - Assessing the Landing Area
  - Water Landings
- Chapter 6: Oral Exam Preparation Questions (question numbers listed above) and answers.

12 An Aviator's Field Guide to the **Seaplane Rating**

1.0 hour

Content:

- Checklist usage
- Normal landing
- Crosswind landing
- Glassy water landing
- Rough water landing
- Confined area landing
- Forward slip to a landing*

Completion Standards:

The student will:

- Understand how to make normal, crosswind, glassy water, rough water, and confined area landings in a seaplane.
- Understand how to make a forward slip to a landing.*
- Develop the habit of proper checklist usage.

* This task is required only for private ASES add-on candidates who hold AMEL without ASEL.

(iStock.com/Nicholas Vettorel)

Ground Lesson 5: Beaching, Docking, Emergency Procedures, and Odds and Ends

ACS Tasks Addressed:
  Private: PA.IX.A,* B;† PA.XII.B
  Commercial: CA.IV.M;‡ CA.IX.B;† CA.IX.C‡

Related Oral Exam Prep Questions:
  See Chapter 6, questions 5, 17, 48, 57–61.

Objectives:

- To introduce beaching and docking a seaplane.
- To explain emergency descents in a seaplane.
- To explain power-off emergency water landings in a seaplane.
- To discuss runway takeoffs and landings in an amphibious seaplane. ⌐AMPHIB
- To review any questions the student may have from the course.

Resources:

- FAA-H-8083-23, Chapter 6
- Chapter 5: Study Guide sections:
  - Beaching
  - Docking
  - Runway Operations in Amphibious Seaplanes ⌐AMPHIB
- Chapter 6: Oral Exam Preparation Questions (question numbers listed above) and answers
- Chapter 7: Preparing for the Practical Test

14 An Aviator's Field Guide to the **Seaplane Rating**

1.0–1.5 hours

Content:

- Beaching
- Docking
- Postflight procedures
- Emergency procedures including emergency descent,[*] simulated emergency approach and landing,[†] and power-off 180° accuracy approach and landing[‡]
- Runway takeoffs/landings and taxi
- Review and address unanswered questions

Completion Standards:

The student will:

- Understand how to dock and beach a seaplane, taking wind and current into account.
- Understand what to do after shutdown.
- Understand how to perform an emergency descent,[*] a simulated emergency approach and landing,[†] and a power-off 180° accuracy approach and landing[‡] in a seaplane.
- Understand how to perform runway takeoffs and landings in an amphibious seaplane.
- Understand how to taxi an amphibious seaplane on land.
- Understand the answers to all of the oral exam preparation questions in this manual (Chapter 6).

[*] Required only for all private candidates (ASEL with or without AMEL).

[†] Required for all private candidates (ASEL with or without AMEL) and for commercial candidates who hold AMEL without ASEL.

[‡] Required only for commercial candidates who hold AMEL without ASEL.

(iStock.com/FotografieLink)

Chapter 2—ASES Syllabus **15**

Flight Lesson 1:
Handling the Aircraft in the Air and on the Water

ACS Tasks Addressed:
Private: PA.I.F, G, I; PA.II.A, B, E, F; PA.III.B; PA.IV.A, B
Commercial: CA.I.F, G, I; CA.II.A, B, E, F; CA.III.B; CA.IV.A, B

Objectives:

- To familiarize the student with flying characteristics of a seaplane.
- To teach the student how to taxi a seaplane on the water: idle, step, and plow.

Content:

- Preflight procedures
- Checklist usage
- Runway operations: taxi, takeoff, and landing
- Getting the feel of the aircraft: slow flight, stalls, and steep turns
- Maneuvering on the water
  - Idle taxi
  - Getting on the step
  - Step taxi, with turns
  - Plow taxi turn (walk through)
  - Sailing
- Introduction to water takeoff: instructor demo, student performs with assistance
- Introduction to water landing: instructor demo

1.5 hours

Completion Standards:

The student will:

- Perform appropriate preflight actions.
- Demonstrate proper checklist usage.
- Be able to taxi to, take off from, and land on a runway.
- Be able to idle taxi, get on the step, step taxi including turns, and demonstrate a simulated plow taxi turn.
- Be able to sail power-off to a designated spot.
- Perform a normal water takeoff with assistance.

AMPHIB

(iStock.com/shaunl)

Flight Lesson 2:
Water Takeoffs and Landings—Normal

ACS Tasks Addressed:
Private: PA.II.A, B, E, F; PA.IV.A, B
Commercial: CA.II.A, B, E, F; CA.IV.A, B

Objective:

- To help the student achieve proficiency in making normal water takeoffs and landings.

Content:

- Preflight procedures
- Checklist usage
- Taxiing
- Getting on the step
- Pitch and airspeed management until liftoff
- Airspeed, flap, and power management after liftoff
- Proper seaplane traffic pattern; appropriate actions beginning abeam touchdown point
- Final approach: airspeed, pitch, and power management; checklist on final
- Actions after touchdown

1.5 hours

Completion Standards:

The student will:

- Achieve proficiency in making normal takeoffs and landings.
- Perform proper preflight and after-landing actions.
- Demonstrate proper checklist usage.

(iStock.com/Shansche)

Flight Lesson 3: Water Takeoffs and Landings—the Other Kinds 1.5 hours

ACS Tasks Addressed:
Private: PA.II.A, B, E, F; PA.III.B; PA.IV.G, H, I, J, K, L
Commercial: CA.II.A, B, E, F; CA.III.B; CA.IV.G, H, I, J, K, L

Objective:
- To help the student become proficient in making crosswind, rough water, glassy water, and confined area water landings.

Content:
- Crosswind takeoff and landing
- Rough water takeoff and landing
- Glassy water takeoff and landing
- Confined area takeoff and landing

Completion Standards:

The student will:
- Achieve proficiency in making crosswind, rough water, glassy water, and confined area takeoffs and landings.
- Practice proper seaplane traffic pattern procedures.
- Demonstrate proper checklist usage.

Flight Lesson 4: Beaching, Docking, Emergency Procedures, and Review 1.5 hours

ACS Tasks Addressed:
Private: PA.IX.A;* PA.IX.B;† PA.XII.B
Commercial: CA.IV.M;‡ CA.IX.B;† CA.IX.C;‡ CA.XII.B

Objective:

- To help the student learn how to beach and dock a seaplane.
- To teach the required emergency procedures: emergency descent,* simulated emergency approach and landing,† and power-off 180° accuracy approach and landing.‡
- To review all previous lessons in preparation for the practical test.

Content:

- Beaching
- Docking
- Emergency procedures
  - Emergency descent*
  - Simulated emergency approach and landing†
  - Power-off 180° accuracy approach and landing†
- Flight test practice

(continued)

---

* Required only for all private candidates (ASEL with or without AMEL).

† Required for all private candidates and for commercial candidates who hold AMEL without ASEL.

‡ Required only for commercial candidates who hold AMEL without ASEL.

(iStock.com/Noel Hendrickson)

Flight Lesson 4: Beaching, Docking, Emergency Procedures, and Review *(continued)*

Completion Standards:

The student will be able to:

- Beach and dock a seaplane, taking into account wind and current.
- Perform the emergency procedures required according to the candidate's certificate and rating(s).
- Perform all previous maneuvers to Private or Commercial (as applicable) ACS standards.

(iStock.com/franckreporter)

Chapter 3
Seabird 1850/1850A Data

This chapter provides specifications, limitations, and performance data for the (fictitious) Seabird 1850 and 1850A, and in each section, space is provided for you to fill in the corresponding data for your training aircraft.

Ask your instructor for photocopies or screenshots of the performance tables in the airplane flight manual/float supplement for your training aircraft so you can determine your takeoff and landing distances under pertinent conditions (such as altitude, temperature, headwind, and flap settings).

Note: The specifications, limitations, and performance data for the Seabird 1850 and 1850A are provided only for example purposes; this information is not to be used for flight planning.

Specifications and Limitations

Sources: Airplane flight manual (AFM)/pilot's operating handbook (POH); float supplement

The Seabird 1850/1850A is a (fictitious) six-seat, single-engine, piston-powered, aluminum-skinned monoplane with a strut-braced high wing.

The Seabird 1850 is fitted with (fictitious) Mallard 3000 straight floats rated at 3,000 pounds, and the Seabird 1850A has (fictitious) Mallard 3000A amphibious floats, also rated at 3,000 pounds.

Table 3-1. Aircraft Data and Performance

	Seabird 1850	Seabird 1850A	Your training aircraft
Length (ft)	26	26	
Wingspan (ft)	35	35	
Height (ft)	12	12.5	
Max gross weight (lb)	3,300	3,300	
Basic empty weight (lb)	2,300	2,400	
V_{NE} (KIAS)	165	165	
V_{NO} (KIAS)	145	145	
V_A (KIAS) at MGW	110	110	
V_{FE} (KIAS)	100	100	
$V_{LE} = V_{LO}$ (KIAS)	N/A	165	
V_S flaps 0° (KIAS) at MGW	55	55	
V_S flaps 20° (or your normal water takeoff/landing flap setting) (KIAS)	50	50	
V_S flaps 40° (or your confined area landing flap setting) (KIAS)	45	45	
V_X (KIAS)	65	65	
V_Y (KIAS)	75	75	
V_G recommended (KIAS)	85	85	
Fuel capacity (US gal)/grade (4 gallons unusable)	65/100LL	65/100LL	
Oil capacity (qt)/type	12/100LL	12/100LL	

For example only; not to be used for flight planning.

Table 3-2. Float Specifications

	Mallard 3000	Mallard 3000A	Your training aircraft
Weight (lb)	600	700	
Length (ft)	20	20	
Depth (deck to keel) (ft)	2.0	2.0	
Number of compartments	7	7	
Bow wheel tire	N/A	5.00 x 5; 25 psi	
Main wheel tire	N/A	6.00 x 6; 45 psi	
Hydraulic system capacity (qt)	N/A	1.5	

For example only; not to be used for flight planning.

Performance

Sources: Airplane flight manual (AFM)/pilot's operating handbook (POH); float supplement

Performance Data

Table 3-3. Performance—Specifications

	Seabird 1850	Seabird 1850A	Your training aircraft
Cruising speed (KIAS) 75% power at 5,000 ft	110	105	
Rate of climb @SL, MGW	800	800	
Takeoff distance	*See Table 3-4.*	Land: *See Table 3-12.* Water: *See Table 3-8.*	Straight floats: *See Table 3-5.* Amphib, water: *See Table 3-9.* Amphib, land: *See Table 3-13.*
Landing distance	*See Table 3-6.*	Land: *See Table 3-14.* Water: *See Table 3-10.*	Straight floats: *See Table 3-7.* Amphib, water: *See Table 3-11.* Amphib, land: *See Table 3-15.*

For example only; not to be used for flight planning.

Chapter 3—Seabird 1850/1850A Data **25**

Seabird 1850 Takeoff and Landing Data

Table 3-4. Seabird 1850 Takeoff Data

		Sea level, 59°F		2500 ft, 50°F	
Seabird 1850 Takeoff Data Flaps 20°, lift off at 55 KIAS. Distances in feet.					
Weight (lb)	**Headwind**	**Water run**	**50 ft obstacle**	**Water run**	**50 ft obstacle**
3300	0	900	1400	1200	1800
	10	600	1000	800	1300
3000	0	700	1200	800	1400
	10	500	800	600	900

For example only; not to be used for flight planning.

Enter the corresponding takeoff distances (specify conditions) for your training aircraft in Table 3-5 below.

Table 3-5. Takeoff Data for Your Training Aircraft (straight floats)

		Elevation/temperature:		Elevation/temperature:	
(Enter aircraft) **Takeoff Data** Flaps ___, lift off at ___ KIAS. Distances in feet.					
Weight (lb)	**Headwind**	**Water run**	**50 ft obstacle**	**Water run**	**50 ft obstacle**

26 An Aviator's Field Guide to the **Seaplane Rating**

Table 3-6. Seabird 1850 Landing Data

		Seabird 1850 Landing Data	
		Flaps 20°/40°, power off. Distances in feet.	
		Sea level, 59°F	2500 ft, 50°F
Weight (lb)	Headwind	50 ft obstacle	50 ft obstacle
3300	0	2000/1500	2200/1700

For example only; not to be used for flight planning.

Enter the corresponding landing distances (specify conditions) for your training aircraft in Table 3-7 below.

Table 3-7. Landing Data for Your Training Aircraft (straight floats)

		(Enter aircraft) Landing Data	
		Flaps power . Distances in feet.	
		Elevation/temperature:	Elevation/temperature:
Weight (lb)	Headwind	50 ft obstacle	50 ft obstacle

Chapter 3—Seabird 1850/1850A Data   **27**

Seabird 1850A Takeoff and Landing Data—Water

Table 3-8. Seabird 1850A Takeoff Data, Water

Seabird 1850A Takeoff Data, Water Flaps 20°, lift off at 55 KIAS. Distances in feet.					
		Sea level, 59°F		2500 ft, 50°F	
Weight (lb)	Headwind	Water run	50 ft obstacle	Water run	50 ft obstacle
3300	0	1100	1600	1400	2000
	10	800	1200	1000	1500
3000	0	900	1400	1000	1600
	10	700	1000	800	1100

For example only; not to be used for flight planning.

Enter the corresponding water takeoff distances (specify conditions) for your amphib training aircraft in Table 3-9 below.

Table 3-9. Takeoff Data for Your Amphib Training Aircraft, Water

(Enter aircraft) Takeoff Data, Water Flaps , lift off at KIAS. Distances in feet.					
		Elevation/temperature:		Elevation/temperature:	
Weight (lb)	Headwind	Water run	50 ft obstacle	Water run	50 ft obstacle

Table 3-10. Seabird 1850A Landing Data, Water

		Seabird 1850A Landing Data, Water Flaps 20°/40°, power off. Distances in feet.	
		Sea level, 59°F	2500 ft, 50°F
Weight (lb)	Headwind	50 ft obstacle	50 ft obstacle
3300	0	2000/1500	2200/1700

For example only; not to be used for flight planning.

Enter the corresponding water landing distances (specify conditions) for your amphib training aircraft in Table 3-11 below.

Table 3-11. Landing Data for Your Amphib Training Aircraft, Water

		(Enter aircraft) _____ Landing Data, Water Flaps ____, power ____. Distances in feet.	
		Elevation/temperature: _____	Elevation/temperature: _____
Weight (lb)	Headwind	50 ft obstacle	50 ft obstacle

Chapter 3—Seabird 1850/1850A Data **29**

Seabird 1850A Takeoff and Landing Data—Land

Table 3-12. Seabird 1850A Takeoff Data, Land

		Sea level, 59°F		2500 ft, 50°F	
Seabird 1850A Takeoff Data, Land Flaps 20°, rotate at 55 KIAS. Distances in feet.					
Weight (lb)	**Headwind**	**Ground run**	**50 ft obstacle**	**Ground run**	**50 ft obstacle**
3300	0	900	1400	1100	1700
	10	600	1000	700	1200
3000	0	700	1200	700	1300
	10	500	800	500	800

For example only; not to be used for flight planning.

Enter the corresponding land takeoff distances (specify conditions) for your amphib training aircraft in Table 3-13 below.

Table 3-13. Takeoff Data for Your Amphib Training Aircraft, Land

		Elevation/temperature:		Elevation/temperature:	
(Enter aircraft) **Takeoff Data, Land** Flaps , rotate at KIAS. Distances in feet.					
Weight (lb)	**Headwind**	**Ground run**	**50 ft obstacle**	**Ground run**	**50 ft obstacle**

30 An Aviator's Field Guide to the **Seaplane Rating**

Table 3-14. Seabird 1850A Landing Data, Land

		Seabird 1850A Landing Data, Land Flaps 30°, power off. Distances in feet.	
		Sea level, 59°F	2500 ft, 50°F
Weight (lb)	Headwind	50 ft obstacle	50 ft obstacle
3300	0	1600	1800

For example only; not to be used for flight planning.

Enter the corresponding landing distances (specify conditions) on land for your amphib training aircraft in Table 3-15 below.

Table 3-15. Landing Data for Your Amphib Training Aircraft, Land

		(*Enter aircraft*) _____ **Landing Data, Land** Flaps _____, power _____. Distances in feet.	
		Elevation/temperature: _____	Elevation/temperature: _____
Weight (lb)	Headwind	50 ft obstacle	50 ft obstacle

Chapter 3—Seabird 1850/1850A Data   31

Chapter 4
Checklists: Normal and Emergency

The following checklists cover normal and emergency procedures for both the straight-float Seabird 1850 and the amphibious Seabird 1850A.

Items pertaining only to the amphibious 1850A are identified with an "Amphib" label in the margin. Those items should be ignored by pilots of straight-float seaplanes.

> *Note:* The checklists in this chapter are for the fictitious Seabird 1850/1850A and are provided for example purposes. The checklists for your specific aircraft may be different than those provided below; refer to and follow the FAA-approved checklists for your training aircraft, and the information provided in your aircraft's airplane flight manual (AFM)/pilot's operating handbook (POH).

Normal Procedures

PREFLIGHT

IMSAFE/PAVE.

Brief: Runway length (land) or water run (water takeoff), weather, W/B, fuel, NOTAMS, TFRs, current, water depth.

General: "wide angle" inspection: level, symmetric, skins smooth, leaks?

Float inspection

1. Pump out each compartment. *Too much water? Hydraulic fluid?*

2. Float sheet metal: *dents, cracks, scratches?*

3. Water rudders: *secure, move freely, cables and pulleys intact/lubricated?*

4. Landing gear: *tire condition/inflation (25 psi nose, 45 psi main), struts, hydraulic leak?*

Cabin

1. AROW—IN AIRCRAFT, including amphib supplement to POH.

2. Tach time—RECORD.

3. Control wheel lock—REMOVE.

4. Ignition—OFF.

5. Avionics power—OFF.

6. Master switch—ON.

7. Fuel gauges—CHECK QUANTITY.

8. Master switch—OFF.

9. Fuel shutoff valve—ON.

10. Fuel selector valve—BOTH.

Oil filler door

1. Check oil level—AT LEAST 9 QUARTS.

2. Oil filler cap—SECURE.

3. Fuel strainer drain—DRAIN.

Fuel

1. Before first flight of the day, and after refueling—
   - Fuel selector drain (midline under engine)—DRAIN, check for water.
   - Fuel line quick drain valve (each side, under fuselage)—DRAIN, check for water.
   - Fuel tank sump quick drain valve (under each wing)—DRAIN, check for water.
2. Fuel quantity (each tank)—MEASURE with dipstick and RECORD.
3. Fuel filler caps (each wing)—SECURE.

Left side of fuselage

1. Baggage door—SECURE.

Empennage

1. Control surfaces—FREE, CORRECT, SECURE.

Right wing

1. Sheet metal—SMOOTH.
2. Flap—SECURE.
3. Aileron—FREE, CORRECT, SECURE.
4. Fuel tank vent—CLEAR.

Nose

1. Static port on left side of fuselage—CLEAR.
2. Propeller—CHECK for security, nicks, oil leaks, spinner secure.
3. Induction air filter and fuel pump cooling inlet—CLEAN/CLEAR.
4. Static port on right side of fuselage—CLEAR.

Left wing

1. Sheet metal—SMOOTH.

2. Pitot cover—REMOVE.

3. Fuel tank vent—CLEAR.

4. Stall warning opening—CLEAR.

5. Aileron—FREE, CORRECT, SECURE.

6. Flap—SECURE.

BEFORE STARTING ENGINE

1. Preflight inspection—COMPLETE.

2. Passenger briefing—COMPLETE *including seat belts, fire extinguisher, door/window operation with eyes closed, life jackets, barf bags.*

3. Seats, seat belts—ADJUST, LOCK.

4. Brakes—TEST/SET.

5. Avionics power—OFF.

6. Electrical equipment (except beacon)—OFF.

7. Circuit breakers—IN.

8. Gear selector—

   - DOWN for land takeoff.
   - UP for water takeoff.

9. Water rudders—

   - Operation free/correct—CHECK visually.
   - UP for land takeoff.
   - DOWN for water takeoff.

10. Wing flaps—CHECK all positions, then UP.

11. Cowl flaps—OPEN.

12. Fuel shutoff valve—ON.

13. Fuel selector valve—BOTH.

STARTING ENGINE

1. Throttle—FULL OPEN.
2. Prop—HIGH RPM.
3. Mixture—FULL RICH.
4. Propeller area—CLEAR.
5. Master switch—ON.
6. Auxiliary fuel pump—ON, observe fuel flow 8–10 gph.
   - Cold start: 3–4 seconds.
   - Hot start: 1–2 seconds.
7. Auxiliary fuel pump—OFF.
8. Ignition switch—START.
9. Throttle—1000 RPM.
10. Mixture—LEAN for taxi.
11. Oil pressure—CHECK in green.
12. Ignition grounding—CHECK.
13. Avionics power—ON.
14. Beacon—ON.
15. Nav lights—ON as required.
16. Radios—ON/SET, check ATIS/AWOS.

BEFORE TAKEOFF

1. Seats, seat belts—SECURE.
2. Cabin doors, windows—CLOSED/LOCKED.
3. Flight controls—FREE AND CORRECT.
4. Flight instruments (altimeter, HI, AI)—CHECK/SET.
5. Mixture—RICH.
6. Fuel quantity—CHECK.
7. Fuel shutoff valve—RECHECK ON.
8. Fuel selector valve—RECHECK BOTH.
9. Elevator trim—SET FOR TAKEOFF.
10. Rudder trim—SET.
11. Run-up—Throttle 1700 RPM.
    - Mags—CHECK (<150 RPM drop cach mag, <50 RPM difference).
    - Prop—CYCLE.
    - Vacuum in green—CHECK.
    - Ammeter charging—CHECK.
    - Voltmeter >13V.
12. Throttle—CLOSED, check idle.
13. Throttle—1000 RPM.
14. Throttle friction lock—SET.
15. Mixture—RICH unless high density altitude.
16. Avionics—SET.
17. Wing flaps—SET:
    - 20° for normal water takeoff (40° for rough water).
    - 20° for normal land takeoff.
18. Landing lights—ON.
19. GUMPFARTS. (See Preflight Procedures in Chapter 5.)

TAKEOFF

On Water

1. Landing gear *up*—RECHECK (2 blue lights, pump off).
2. Water rudders—DOWN.
3. Wing flaps 20° (except rough water)—SET.
4. Cowl flaps open—RECHECK.
5. Control wheel—HOLD FULL AFT.
6. Throttle—FULL (advance smoothly).
7. Water rudders—UP then hand back to throttle.
8. Control wheel—PITCH DOWN to planing attitude (5–8° nose up) when nose stops rising.
9. Airspeed—50–55 KIAS.
10. Control wheel—APPLY LIGHT BACK-PRESSURE to lift off, then pitch level to accelerate to V_X (65 KIAS) in ground effect.

    If won't lift off despite flying airspeed (heavy/glassy/ rough), lift one float, or jerk flaps to full then back to 20° after liftoff.
11. Climb speed—65 KIAS until clear of obstacles straight ahead.
12. Flaps—REDUCE TO 10°.
13. Airspeed—V_Y (75 KIAS)
14. Power—24", 2500 RPM.
15. Flaps—REDUCE to 0° and LOCK.

On Land

1. Water rudders—UP.
2. Wing flaps—20°.
3. Cowl flaps—OPEN.
4. Throttle—FULL (advance smoothly).
5. Control wheel—PITCH UP to keep nose wheels just off runway.
6. Airspeed—50–55 KIAS, let it fly off with no increase in pitch.
7. Control wheel—PITCH LEVEL to accelerate to V_X (65 KIAS) in ground effect, then pitch to maintain V_X until clear of obstacle straight ahead.
8. Landing gear—UP as soon as climb is established. "Positive rate, gear UP."
9. Flaps—REDUCE to 10°.
10. Airspeed—V_Y (75 KIAS).
11. Flaps—REDUCE to 0° and LOCK.

NORMAL CLIMB

1. Airspeed—85 KIAS.
2. Power—24", 2500 RPM.
3. Mixture—RICH.
4. Cowl flaps—OPEN.

CRUISE

1. Power—20-21", 2500 RPM.
2. Cowl flaps—OPEN.
3. Stabilizer trim—SET.
4. Mixture—LEAN as needed.
5. Gear indicators—RECHECK UP (handle, 2 blue lights/ pump off, red tabs on floats, mirrors).
6. Landing light—OFF.

DESCENT

1. Fuel selector—BOTH.

2. Power—SAME AS CRUISE.

3. Mixture—RICHEN.

4. Cowl flaps—OPEN.

5. Landing light—ON.

BEFORE LANDING

On Water

1. Landing gear—UP by all indicators (gear lever, 2 blue lights and pump off, red tabs on floats, mirrors, gear advisory warning).

2. Water rudders—UP.

3. Fuel shutoff valve—OPEN.

4. Fuel tank selector—BOTH.

5. Altitude—500 ft AGL until on final.

6. Landing area—SURVEY (wind direction/strength, obstructions, depth, traffic, dock approach).

7. Throttle—REDUCE to 15" abeam touchdown spot.

8. Airspeed—SLOW to white arc.

9. Flaps—20°.

10. Throttle—as needed to maintain 75 KIAS; generally 13–15" on final.

11. Propeller—FULL FORWARD (high RPM) on final.

12. Landing gear—RECHECK UP on final.

13. *Check, and then say out loud:* "Mixture rich, prop full forward, gear is *UP* for water landing."

On Land

1. Landing gear—DOWN by all indicators (gear lever, 2 yellow lights and pump off, red tabs on floats, mirrors, gear advisory warning).

2. Water rudders—UP.

3. Fuel shutoff valve—OPEN.

4. Fuel tank selector—BOTH.

5. Altitude—500 ft AGL until on final.

6. Throttle—REDUCE to 15" abeam touchdown spot.

7. Airspeed—SLOW to white arc.

8. Flaps—30° (40° if rear seat passengers).

9. Throttle—as needed to maintain 75 KIAS; generally 13–15" on final.

10. Propeller—FULL FORWARD (high RPM) on final.

11. Landing gear—RECHECK DOWN on final.

12. *Check, and then say out loud:* "Mixture rich, prop full forward, gear is *DOWN* for runway landing."

LANDING

On Water

1. Touchdown—SLIGHT PITCH UP (8° approx.); *never* level or pitch down.

Step Taxi

2. Power—2000–2100 RPM.

3. Pitch—Nearly level, approx. 5° nose up.

Idle Taxi

4. Power—1000 RPM or less.

5. Control wheel—FULL AFT unless taxiing downwind.

6. Water rudders—DOWN.

7. Floats—WATCH BOW AND STERN for submersion while taxiing.

On Land

1. Touchdown—PITCH UP (8° approx.); touch down on main gear, **never** on nose wheels.

2. Power—1000–1200 RPM.

3. Control wheel—EASE BACK PRESSURE; let nose wheels settle gently to runway.

4. Braking—MINIMUM.

When clear of the runway

5. Throttle—1000 RPM.

6. Mixture—LEAN for taxi.

7. Flaps—UP.

8. Transponder—STANDBY.

9. Landing light—OFF.

AFTER LANDING

Docking

1. Approach—INTO WIND if possible.

2. Seat belt—UNBUCKLE.

3. Avionics power—OFF.

4. Lights, electrical equipment—OFF except beacon.

5. Master switch—OFF.

6. Magnetos—RIGHT OR LEFT instead of both, if needed to reduce speed.

7. Headset—ON GLARESHIELD, cord hung on side light so not in way as you exit.

8. Window—OPEN (in case the door locks shut).

9. Right hand—on mixture, not on control wheel.

10. Mixture—FULL LEAN to shut down engine when dock is "made."

11. Magnetos—OFF.

(continued)

Chapter 4—Checklists: Normal and Emergency **43**

12. Door—OPEN.

13. Left foot—OUT, on step.

14. Right foot—ON RUDDER to steer.

When tied up, RETURN TO FLIGHT DECK.

15. Mixture, mags, master—RECHECK OFF.

16. Seat belts—BUCKLE so they don't get locked out and bang up the side of the aircraft in flight.

17. Window—Leave OPEN.

18. Fuel selector—RIGHT OR LEFT.

Securing On Land

1. Avionics power—OFF.

2. Lights, electrical equipment—OFF.

3. Mixture—FULL LEAN.

4. Magnetos—OFF.

5. Master switch—OFF.

6. Seat belts—BUCKLE.

7. Fuel selector valve—RIGHT OR LEFT.

8. Elevator trim—TAKEOFF.

9. Overall—INSPECT: *fuel/oil leaks? scratches/dents? asymmetry?*

AFTER OPERATING IN WATER

1. Floats—PUMP OUT: *excessive water (which compartment[s])? hydraulic fluid?*

2. Exterior—RINSE with fresh water. ***Rinse very thoroughly after operating in salt water, especially tail section.***

3. Float pulleys, elevator hinges, elevator pushrod pivot, water rudder fittings—LUBRICATE.

Selected Emergency Procedures

ENGINE FAILURE

Engine Failure During Takeoff Run (On Water)

1. Throttle—IDLE.
2. Control wheel—FULL AFT.
3. Mixture—IDLE CUT-OFF.
4. Ignition switch—OFF.
5. Master switch—OFF.

Engine Failure During Takeoff Roll (On Land)

1. Throttle—IDLE.
2. Brakes—APPLY.
3. Wing flaps—RETRACT.
4. Mixture—IDLE CUT-OFF.
5. Ignition switch—OFF.
6. Master switch—OFF.

AMPHIB

Engine Failure in Flight (partial or complete loss of power)

1. Airspeed—85 KIAS.
2. Landing gear—UP.
3. Flaps—UP.
4. Heading—Turn *immediately* toward landing area.
5. Mixture—RICH.
6. Fuel selector—BOTH.
7. Ignition—BOTH.

AMPHIB

If engine does not restart and power loss is complete, use the POWER-OFF LANDING checklist below.

Chapter 4—Checklists: Normal and Emergency   **45**

POWER-OFF LANDING

1. Complete ENGINE FAILURE IN FLIGHT checklist above.

When committed to land (into the wind if possible):

2. Airspeed—85 KIAS until very short final.

3. Mixture—IDLE CUT-OFF.

4. Fuel shutoff valve—OFF.

5. Ignition switch—OFF.

6. Master switch—OFF.

7. Water rudders—UP.

8. Landing gear—Confirm UP by all indicators for water landing.

   If landing on land, gear should remain up if landing area is soft or rough, but can be extended if landing area is firm and smooth.

9. Flaps—EXTEND to 40° if able to do so while maintaining control.

10. Doors/windows—UNLATCH.

11. Pitch—Normal landing attitude.

LANDING GEAR MALFUNCTIONS

Landing Gear Fails to Retract (as indicated by one or more of the gear position indicators)

1. Master switch—ON.

2. Landing gear handle—CHECK FULL UP.

3. Landing gear motor circuit breaker—IN.

4. Landing gear handle—DOWN, then UP.

5. Landing gear motor—CHECK OPERATION ("gear in transit" light, ammeter, and sound).

If the landing gear still does not indicate UP by all indicators:

6. Landing gear motor circuit breaker—PULL.

7. Landing gear handle—RECHECK UP.

8. Emergency hand pump selector valve—GEAR UP position.

9. Emergency hand pump—PUMP until gear locks in UP position.

10. Gear up lights—CHECK ILLUMINATED.

11. Mechanical gear position indicators (on top of floats), mirror, direct observation of nose gear position—VISUALLY CHECK in UP position.

Landing Gear Fails to Extend

1. Master switch—ON.

2. Landing gear handle—CHECK FULL DOWN.

3. Landing gear motor circuit breaker—IN.

4. Mechanical gear position indicators—VISUALLY CHECK (on top of floats).

5. Landing gear handle—UP, then DOWN.

6. Landing gear motor—CHECK OPERATION ("gear in transit" light, ammeter, and sound).

If landing gear still does not indicate DOWN by all indicators:

7. Landing gear motor circuit breaker—PULL.

8. Landing gear handle—RECHECK DOWN.

9. Emergency hand pump selector valve—GEAR DOWN position.

10. Emergency hand pump—PUMP until gear locks in DOWN position.

(continued)

11. Gear down lights—CHECK ILLUMINATED.

12. Mechanical gear position indicators (on top of floats), mirror, and direct observation of nose gear position—VISUALLY CHECK in DOWN position.

Gear Up Landing (On Land)

1. Landing gear—CHECK UP by all indicators.

2. Runway—Grass (ideally wet) or smooth ground.

3. Flaps—40° on final approach.

4. Airspeed—70 KIAS on final approach.

5. Touchdown—Normal landing attitude.

6. Control wheel—FULL AFT after touchdown.

ELECTRICAL SYSTEM MALFUNCTIONS

Excessive Rate of Charge (ammeter shows full scale [+] deflection)

1. Alternator—OFF.

2. Alternator circuit breaker—PULL.

3. Nonessential electrical equipment—OFF.

4. LAND as soon as practical.

Ammeter Indicates Discharge

1. Avionics power switch—OFF.

2. Alternator circuit breaker—CHECK IN.

3. Master switch—OFF (both halves).

4. Master switch—ON (both halves).

5. Avionics power switch—ON.

If ammeter still shows discharge (–):

6. Alternator—OFF.

7. Nonessential radio and electrical equipment—OFF.

8. LAND as soon as practical.

48 An Aviator's Field Guide to the **Seaplane Rating**

Chapter 5
Study Guide

The Briefest Seaplane History Lesson *Ever*

The first seaplane flew only seven years after the Wright brothers' first powered flight at Kitty Hawk in 1903. History does not record (as far as I know) whether the early development of seaplanes was driven more by the fact that there were far more waterways than runways in the early days of aviation, or by early pilots' thinking, "Flying is amazing, but you know what would *really* be cool? Taking off and landing *on the water!*" Regardless, the development of seaplanes progressed at least as fast as that of land planes at the dawn of aviation. For example, the first Boeing aircraft (in 1916) was a seaplane, and seaplanes saw military service in World War I. In the 1920s, seaplane development progressed rapidly, and by the late 1920s and early 1930s, world airspeed records were dominated by seaplanes. In the 1930s, large flying boats such as the Boeing 314 Clipper were in use for long-range passenger service. While World War II effectively ended long-range seaplane passenger service, seaplanes including the famous Consolidated PBY Catalina served in a variety of roles in World War II.

In the post-war era, long-range passenger service was taken over by jets. Today, seaplanes remain in use for short-range passenger service, both scheduled and charter, in coastal areas. Many light seaplanes are primarily used for recreation, but others are working aircraft, with roles (in addition to passenger transportation/charter) including firefighting, search and rescue, wildlife management, fishing charters, servicing inshore oil rigs, and missionary service.

And some, like the aircraft you're about to fly, are used to train the next generation of seaplane pilots. Fewer than 6 percent of pilots in the United States have their seaplane rating, and only a small minority of those with seaplane ratings are active seaplane pilots, so you are about to join a pretty exclusive group.

Seaplane Basics

Seaplanes come in two varieties: flying boats and floatplanes.

The bottom of a flying boat's fuselage is shaped like the hull of a boat, and the fuselage itself floats on the water. Lateral stability while on the water is provided by small pontoons mounted under the wingtips. Most flying boats have retractable landing gear to allow runway operations. Flying boats include the Lake amphibians, the Grumman Goose and Mallard, and the currently produced Progressive Aerodyne SeaRey, ICON A5, and Super Petrel amphibious light-sport aircraft.

Floatplanes, on the other hand, are land planes with two floats and supporting structures attached. (Some operators convert their floatplanes seasonally by removing the floats and replacing them with skis or conventional wheel landing gear.) Floatplanes are either *straight* or *amphibious* (amphib). Straight floats have no wheels, so straight floatplanes are made to be operated exclusively from the water. (They are launched and retrieved by purpose-built forklift-like vehicles so that they can be stored on land between flights.) Amphibious floats, on the other hand, have wheel landing gear that can be retracted for water takeoffs and landings and extended for runway landings and takeoffs.

In general, straight floatplanes are lighter than amphibs, have better performance on the water (including shorter takeoff distances), and are a little faster in the air. Straight floatplanes are most common in areas where aviation fuel is readily available on the water, such as Alaska. In most of the United States, however, aviation fuel is not available on the water, so amphibious floats, despite their performance penalties, are a necessity to allow runway landing for refueling.

The ability to operate an aircraft from water seems magical at times, but the weight and drag of floats does take a toll on performance: A single-engine floatplane may cruise 30 knots slower than the same aircraft without hundreds of pounds of floats and the associated maze of struts and cables. If you have hundreds of miles to go, a seaplane would not be your first choice as a way to get there—unless, of course, your destination is, say, a cabin on a remote lake, in which case a seaplane is the *only* way to go.

Transitioning to Water Flying: What to Expect

A seaplane flies like a regular airplane. No new techniques are needed, but you will need to pay more attention to the rudder pedals than you may be used to doing in land planes for coordinated flight. Seaplanes (and especially floatplanes) have much more drag than land planes to begin with; flying seaplanes in a slip or a skid further degrades performance by adding a significant amount of extra form drag, as you are presenting a huge surface area (the sides of the floats and supporting structures) to the relative wind as you slip or skid. This may adversely affect yaw stability, which is why some seaplanes have a small ventral fin on the bottom of the tail section, and some have vertical fins at the outboard ends of the horizontal stabilizer. And even in coordinated flight, in addition to the reduction in cruising speed, you will find the power-off descent rate of a seaplane to be impressive. Do not reduce power to idle unless you really need to descend fast, or until you are inches above the water (or runway) and are ready to land. In general, when reducing power in a floatplane, reduce it gradually.

While flying a seaplane is much like flying a land plane, operating a seaplane on the water is a whole different ballgame. Much of your ASES training will be about learning how to taxi, take off, and land on the water. Your instructor will address the details of all of those activities in the course of your training, but in general, one of the biggest differences to note between land planes and seaplanes is that seaplanes tend to weathervane—i.e., point into the wind—when on the water. Regardless of where you want the plane to go while on the water, it will want to head to windward. Because of this,

Chapter 5—Study Guide **51**

seaplanes have water rudders, which can be retracted in flight and extended while on the water, to help with directional control while idle taxiing.

Keep in mind also that seaplanes have no brakes; therefore, careful planning is needed when approaching a dock, ramp, or beach.

And while on the water, you will need to be attentive at all times to the wind direction and have the ailerons and elevator positioned properly for the wind. (The general guidance, which you are likely familiar with from flying land planes, is to "climb into the wind, dive away from the wind," and in most situations this guidance works for seaplanes as well. The exceptions are that while idle taxiing, you will generally keep the stick in your lap unless taxiing downwind, and while step taxiing, the ailerons will always be held in the direction of your turn.)

For amphibs only: In addition to the differences between landplanes and seaplanes generally, amphibious seaplanes introduce another challenge, and it is a significant one. As with a land plane, the landing gear must be down for landing on a runway; this is routine for pilots with experience in complex aircraft. The challenge is this: In an amphibious seaplane, the landing gear absolutely must be *UP* when landing on the water—*every single time*, without exception.

To land a seaplane gear up on the runway will be expensive, but the likelihood of injury is minimal. But to land an amphibious seaplane on the water with the landing gear down can be—and often is—fatal, as the aircraft will often pitchpole and end up inverted. Pilots and passengers may be severely injured by striking the control wheel, instrument panel, or windscreen due to the initial sudden deceleration upon touching down on the water with the gear down, but even if one survives and is conscious, underwater egress from an inverted, sinking aircraft is difficult at best and may be impossible.

52 An Aviator's Field Guide to the **Seaplane Rating**

But think about this: If you raise the landing gear after every takeoff, the only way you can make a gear-down water landing (other than by deliberately extending the gear at some point during the flight) is if there is a failure of whatever system holds your landing gear in the retracted position (mechanical uplocks, hydraulic pressure). The Seaplane Pilots Association reviewed 10 years of data regarding amphibious seaplane accidents and found that in 83 percent of cases of gear-down water landings, the cause of the accident was the pilot's failure to raise the landing gear after takeoff. The study also found that one in four gear-down water landings are fatal.

A tragic story of the consequences of landing on the water with the landing gear down is told in the AOPA Air Safety Institute video "No Greater Burden: Surviving an Aircraft Accident" (about 31 minutes long).[1] I encourage you to watch it—not to scare you, but to indelibly impress on you that it is absolutely essential that the landing gear be up *every single time* for water landings. In your amphibious seaplane training, you will form habits that will help prevent you from ever making this mistake.

The key habits are these:

1. Your first action after every takeoff—before retracting flaps, before reducing power, before calling ATC, and even if you are just staying in the pattern for a touch-and-go—must be to retract the landing gear as soon as you are climbing. "Positive rate, GEAR UP."

2. Verify your landing gear position at least three times before landing: on downwind, on base, and on final. My personal habit for final approach—every single time—is to check, and then say out loud, "Gear is UP for water landing" (or "Gear is DOWN for runway landing").

---

[1] Air Safety Institute, "No Greater Burden: Surviving an Aircraft Accident," May 1, 2015, YouTube video, 31:26, https://www.youtube.com/watch?v=8bjsxBEVl5o.

3. In an aircraft with side-by-side seating, it is difficult to see the landing gear position indicators on the top of the float on the other side without unbuckling your seat belt, so use your right-seat passenger if you have one. Teach them how to interpret the mechanical gear position indicators, and have them confirm for you the position of the right landing gear by calling out, "Landing gear indicates UP," or whatever language you agree on.[2]

Helpful educational resources offered by the Seaplane Pilots Association to encourage and enhance safe operations within the seaplane community include its "Amphibious Aircraft Gear Management Best Practices" document and "Safe Amphibious Gear Operations" video, both available on its website (seaplanepilotsassociation.org).[3]

Are We Flying, or Are We Boating?

The answer is *yes*: We are in effect doing both when we operate a seaplane.

A seaplane is an aircraft while in the air, subject to all the same FAA regulations as any other aircraft: 14 CFR Part 61, Part 91, Part 135, etc. But while on the water, it's a watercraft and must obey the same right-of-way and navigation rules as other watercraft. These rules are codified in COLREGS (International Regulations for Preventing Collisions at Sea), which govern watercraft outside of a published demarcation line that closely follows the shoreline, and in the U.S. Inland Navigation Rules if inshore of that demarcation line. These nearly identical sets of rules define, among other things, the right-of-way hierarchy on the water—that is, what kind of vessel has the right-of-way if two vessels are on a collision course. The rationale for this pecking order is that *the less maneuverable vessel has the right-of-way.*

---

[2] Lacey Panepinto of Southern Seaplane, Inc., personal communication with author, January 13, 2025.

[3] "Amphibious Aircraft Gear Management Best Practices," Seaplane Pilots Association, accessed February 4, 2025, https://seaplanepilotsassociation.org/wp-content/uploads/Amphib-Safety-final-6-14-2022-1.pdf; Seaplane Pilots Association, "Safe Amphibious Gear Operations," video, https://seaplanepilotsassociation.org/online-training/.

Seaplanes on the water—taxiing, taking off, or landing—are deemed to be the *most* maneuverable of all watercraft, so with rare exceptions, **all other vessels on the water should be considered to have right-of-way over seaplanes**. This means that seaplanes should remain clear of, and give way to, all other vessels. (14 CFR §91.115 reiterates this from the FAA's perspective.) As seaplane pilots, this does not mean that the lake must be empty for us to land on it, but it does mean that we must plan our approach and our departure carefully so as to remain clear of all other vessels (including any skiers or floats that a boat may be towing, sometimes on a long line).

Many, if not all, states have their own regulations regarding the right-of-way of vessels on the water, and some address seaplanes specifically. It is worth looking up state regulations in states in which you operate a seaplane, but none are more restrictive than §91.115.

Regarding right-of-way on the water, three specific situations deserve mention: *crossing, meeting,* and *overtaking.*

- Crossing—If two vessels are on headings such that their paths will cross, and the vessels may collide when the paths cross (i.e., they're on a collision course that is not head-on), *the vessel on the other's right has the right-of-way* (even if it happens to be a seaplane).

- Meeting—If two vessels (of any type) are headed directly toward one another on reciprocal courses on the water, *each vessel must alter its course to its right.*

- Overtaking—If a faster vessel is overtaking a slower vessel on the same course, *the overtaking vessel must give way to the vessel being overtaken* (regardless of the type of vessel), and the overtaking vessel must alter its course so as to pass the other vessel either on the right or on the left.

Therefore, 14 CFR §91.115 notwithstanding, there are situations in which a seaplane may have the right-of-way. For example, if a seaplane and a boat are proceeding at right angles to one another, and the seaplane is on the right of the other vessel, the seaplane technically has the right-of-way. And if a speedboat is overtaking an idle-taxiing seaplane, the seaplane technically has the right-of-way.

Chapter 5—Study Guide **55**

Finally, a seaplane sailing power-off is absolutely less maneuverable than any powerboat and than most sailboats, so in that situation the seaplane would very likely be ruled to have the right-of-way over those more maneuverable vessels.

Nevertheless, in almost all circumstances, even if you think the rules may give you the right-of-way, the smart choice is to give way whenever you are able.

A final note regarding right-of-way: If one seaplane is on final approach for landing and another is taxiing on the water or taking off, the seaplane that is on the water or taking off has the right-of-way, because it is deemed to be less maneuverable.

Regarding navigation, many waterways (including the intracoastal waterway) have channels marked by red and green markers positioned so that the red markers will be on the right and the green markers on the left for a vessel returning to a harbor via a river or channel, or traveling clockwise (i.e., southward on the U.S. East Coast) in the Intracoastal Waterway. While taxiing on the water, seaplane pilots are required to obey the same channel markers as other watercraft as well as to obey "No Wake Zone" markers. Lakes may have their own areas with speed limits or areas where certain types of vessels (sometimes including seaplanes) are not allowed.

Aside from issues of right-of-way and navigational markers, there is also a fair amount of boating terminology associated with seaplanes. Each float is really a kind of boat, with a hull, deck, keel, skeg (on straight floats), rudder, bow, and stern (see Figure 5-1). In cross section, the hull of a seaplane float is generally V-shaped or fluted. While taxiing at slow speeds, the seaplane float is a displacement hull, like a rowboat or sailboat, or a powerboat at low speed. However, as the seaplane accelerates during the takeoff run, it transitions from moving *through* the water to planing *on the surface* of the water like a ski boat (and like the water skier): The seaplane is now referred to as being "on the step."

Like a boat, floats leak and must be pumped out with a bilge pump of a type boaters are familiar with. Each float is divided by bulkheads into several compartments (seven in the case of the Seabird 1850's Mallard 3000 floats), each of which needs to be pumped out individually after flights involving water landings, as well as after the

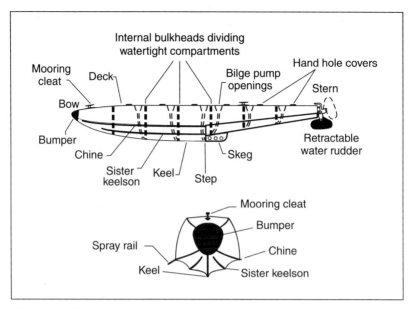

Figure 5-1. Float components. *(FAA-H-8083-23)*

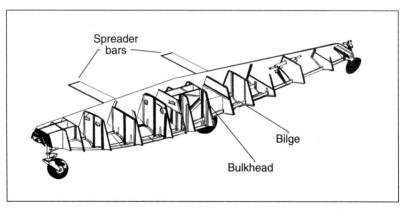

Figure 5-2. Float cross section.

seaplane has sat in the water for more than an hour or so (see Figure 5-2). (Seaplane floats are required to have at least four compartments; the rationale is that if one compartment is ruptured—by debris in the water, or by rocks on a beach, for example—water will be taken on only by that one compartment while the others remain intact.) Float certification requires that a float still floats with two compartments flooded—but don't rely on this.

A) Cleat Hitch

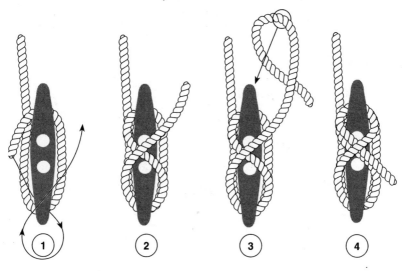

B) Two Half Hitches

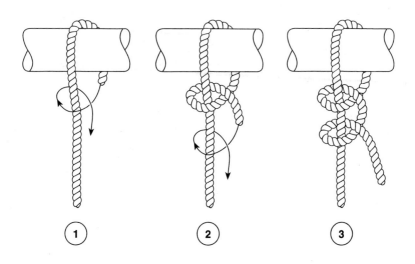

Figure 5-3. Useful knots for securing a seaplane: (A) cleat hitch, (B) two half hitches, (C) taut line hitch, and (D) bowline.
(*A, B, D: Based on illus. by Jan – stock.adobe.com*)

C) Taut Line Hitch

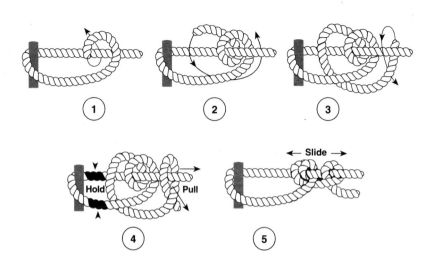

D) Bowline

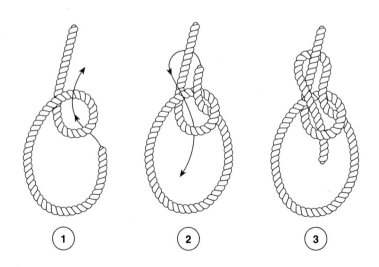

Chapter 5—Study Guide

Seaplane floats are rated for a certain displacement, meaning the weight of the water they displace when floating at their design waterline (for example, 3,000 pounds for the Mallard 3000 floats, though the float model number is not always the same as the float's certificated weight rating). Each float (not the two floats combined) is required to be able to support 90 percent of the aircraft's maximum gross weight. The mathematical upshot of this is that to find the maximum aircraft weight that a set of floats will support, divide the float's weight rating by 0.9. Therefore, in the case of the Mallard 3000 floats, the maximum aircraft gross weight is 3,333 pounds.

Some seaplane pilots, using nautical terminology, refer to the left float as the port side float and the right float as the starboard float, but most simply refer to them as the left float and the right float.

Like sailors, we refer to the direction the wind is coming from as "windward" and the downwind direction as "leeward." So, as examples of how the terms are used, a seaplane's weathervane tendency makes it point to *windward*, and it is often easier to leave a dock from the *leeward* side.

Like boats, seaplanes carry dock lines, which are attached to cleats bolted to the decks and are used for tying up to docks. At a minimum, you should learn a few knots needed to secure your seaplane to a dock and/or a piling, including a cleat hitch and either two half hitches or a taut line hitch. A bowline is very handy for creating a loop in a line. (See Figure 5-3 on pages 58–59.) (Your instructor can teach you these knots, and likely others as well.) Some seaplane pilots carry an anchor aboard their aircraft, either for short stops on the water for lunch or fishing or to help secure the aircraft on a beach. And seaplanes carry a paddle attached to the float, in case you overestimate how far you can coast after shutting down the engine while approaching a dock.

In this course, you will learn how to "sail" in a seaplane, though it is different from sailing a boat. We will cover more details about this later in this chapter.

60 An Aviator's Field Guide to the **Seaplane Rating**

And finally, as a seaplane pilot, you will need to be at least as attentive as a sailor to the wind—its speed, its direction, and how it is affecting the water surface. In the vast majority of the places you will be landing and taking off from, there is no ATIS/AWOS, so you will have to learn how to determine wind speed and direction yourself from the air by looking at the water surface and other available clues. And if you operate in rivers or tidal areas, you will have to consider the effects of current (discussed in further detail later in this chapter).

Reading the Water Surface

Your observations of the water surface and surroundings—from the air before landing, or from the dock before takeoff—can help you make your own determination of the speed and direction of the wind.

Clues to Wind Speed

- What the water looks like (see Figure 5-4 and Table 5-1 on page 62).
  A few key takeaways from this table:
  - Glassy water surface when wind up to 2–3 knots.
  - Ripples alone when wind from 2–3 knots to 7–8 knots.
  - Wind streaks start at about 7–8 knots.
  - Whitecaps start at about 13 knots.
  - Above 20 knots, stay home.

- Flags—There are various formulas and guidelines, but generally if the flag is not moving, the wind speed is less than 10 knots, and if the flag is waving its entire length, the wind speed is at least in the high teens (knots).

- Smoke—The lighter the breeze, the more vertically smoke rises.

- ATIS/AWOS at a nearby airport.

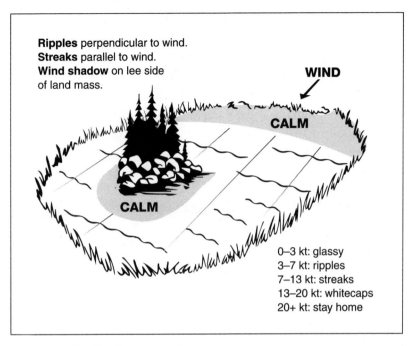

Figure 5-4. Reading the water surface.

Table 5-1. Wind Speed and Water Surface Conditions

Wind speed (kt)	Surface conditions
0–3	Glassy, possibly a few small ripples
3–7	Small waves (ripples), but no wind streaks
7–13	Small waves (ripples) with wind streaks but few if any whitecaps
13–20	Rough. Wind streaks, whitecaps, but no "frothing" (foamy) whitecaps thrown from wave crests
21+	Large waves with frothing whitecaps. This is at or above the capability of most light seaplanes (and their pilots!). If you must land or take off in these conditions, be certain that you are headed directly into the wind. Use rough water technique. Do not try to taxi downwind: sail instead.

(Adapted from instruction given by Rich Hensch of Florida Seaplanes, Inc.; adapted by him from the Beaufort Wind Scale and the National Weather Service Wind Scale.)

Clues to Wind Direction

The water surface appearance and other clues can provide indications of wind direction (see Figure 5-4).

- *Ripples*—The wind is always *perpendicular* to ripples.

- *Streaks*—The wind is always *parallel* to streaks.

- *Wind shadow*—Water adjacent to the lee shore of an island or land mass will be calm and glassy, so that is the downwind or leeward side of the island.

- *Flags and smoke*—Both give an indication not only of direction but also of speed.

- *ATIS/AWOS at a nearby airport*—Note, however, that because of differences in local geography (e.g., hills, etc.), the wind at your intended landing site may be very different from the nearby airport's ATIS/AWOS, even if the airport is only a few miles away.

Assessing the Landing Area

When flying a seaplane, there is usually no one to tell you whether or where it's safe to land. You determine the location and direction of your "runway" yourself based on wind, the water surface, and geography. You alone have to decide whether the path is clear of power lines, other vessels, shallow debris, sandbars, or other obstructions; whether the water is deep enough; whether the waves are too big; and whether you have enough room to land and (especially) enough room to take off.

Satellite photos—including those available on Google Maps and Google Earth—are quite helpful in assessing the area before you take off. Both Google Maps and Google Earth have measuring tools that will help you determine whether the body of water is long enough for you to land and take off. (Keep in mind the possibility that conditions such as water levels may have changed since the photos were taken.) The resolution of the satellite photos in ForeFlight is in my experience not quite as good as Google Maps/Google Earth

Chapter 5—Study Guide **63**

when zoomed in, but the measuring tool in ForeFlight is much easier to use than the one in Google Maps and Google Earth, and it shows distances in feet, which makes it easier to judge (without having to convert miles to feet) whether you'll have enough room to land and take off.

Whenever possible, call ahead and speak with someone familiar with current local conditions, and even better, with someone who has experience flying floats in that area. Even after having done all of that, *always* fly over the intended landing area at 500 feet to assess it before landing.

Regarding determining available takeoff or landing distance without Google Earth or ForeFlight: Let's say you want 3,000 feet to feel comfortable getting onto and off of a lake. A low cruise setting of 21"/2300 RPM in the Seabird 1850/1850A will give you about 100 knots, and that's 169 feet per second. At 169 feet per second, it takes about 18 seconds to fly 3,000 feet, so you can use the time required to fly across the lake at a known speed as a yardstick for how much water you have: Measure the number of seconds it takes to fly over the landing area at 100 knots and multiply that number of seconds by 169 to find the number of feet available. (You can work out the math for other speeds.)

Satellite photos can also help you choose in advance a landmark to use as your *abort point* for takeoff or landing—a point by which you must have lifted off if taking off, or touched down if landing. If the aircraft is not off the water by that point on takeoff, you abort the takeoff. When landing, if you haven't touched down by that point, you abort the landing and go around. This abort point should be part of every pre-takeoff briefing (even if only silently, to yourself) and every before-landing briefing.

Preflight Procedures

(See the Seabird's Normal Procedures checklist in Chapter 4 of this book, and your training aircraft's Normal Procedures checklist.)

- **IMSAFE** to assess your personal readiness for flight—Illness, **M**edications, **S**tress, **A**lcohol, **F**atigue, and **E**xternal factors.

- **PAVE** to assess the *risk elements* for the flight:
  - the **P**ilot (IMSAFE addresses this.)
  - the **A**ircraft.
  - the en**V**ironment.
  - **E**xternal factors, including "get-home-itis" and pressure from passengers.

- Wind, wave height, runway length (land/water), obstructions including power lines, docking/beaching options. (*Sources:* Google Maps, Google Earth, ForeFlight satellite view measuring tool, call ahead for local knowledge, request current ground level photos of the dock.)

- Preflight inspection—Same as for land plane, except for float inspection/pumpout:
  - If aircraft is in the water, you may need to turn it around to complete preflight inspection of the other side.

- Passenger briefing—**SAFE**:
  - **S**eatbelt operation; **S**econd pair of eyes: for traffic and for landing gear position indicators.
  - **A**ir controls: cabin heat, cabin air; **A**irsickness bags.
  - **F**ire extinguisher location and operation.
  - **E**gress (how to operate doors and windows by feel, *with eyes closed*); **E**mergency equipment (including life jackets and survival kit); **E**mergency procedures.

- Self-briefing:
  - Exit plan from dock or beach (if someone is available to help, *use them*).
  - Planned takeoff direction.
  - Abort point.
  - Altitude needed before turning back to the lake if engine fails.

- Engine start:
  - Be ready: Once you start the engine on the water, you're moving.
  - For engine start procedure, see checklist.

Chapter 5—Study Guide **65**

- Taxi:
  - On land (*amphib only*):
    - › Use brake steering.
    - › Hold controls appropriately for wind ("climb into the wind, dive away from the wind").
  - On water (idle taxi; other types discussed below):
    - › Water rudders down as soon as engine starts.
    - › *Max 1000 RPM*: More power will submerge the bows of the floats.
    - › Watch bows and sterns of floats at all times.
    - › Hold ailerons appropriately for wind; stick in lap, except forward if taxiing downwind.

- Run-up—*Quickly, to minimize spray damage to prop*:
  - Mags, prop, ammeter, vacuum. 10 seconds or less.

- Before takeoff on water—Use a checklist mnemonic appropriate to your training aircraft. GUMPFARTS works well for the Seabird, but *use whatever mnemonic your instructor recommends.*
  - **GUMPFARTS** (used at Florida Seaplanes[4]):
    - › **G**as: fuel selector on BOTH, fuel pump as required.
    - › **U**ndercarriage: gear UP (*amphib only*).
    - › **M**ixture: best power.
    - › **P**rop: full forward.
    - › **F**laps: set for takeoff (20° in Seabird).
    - › **A**rea clear of traffic (boaters or aircraft) and obstructions, including power lines.
    - › (Water) **R**udders: UP.
    - › **T**rim: SET for takeoff.
    - › **S**tick (control wheel): full aft.

- Getting on the step:
  - Full power, stick full aft.
  - Water rudders UP, then hand back to throttle.

---

[4] Florida Seaplanes, https://www.flyfloatplanes.com/.

- When nose stops rising, pitch to approximately 5° up, trim out control pressures.
- If taking off, keep power full.
- If not taking off, reduce power to approximately 20" MP/2500 RPM (prop full forward) to stay on step.

Step taxi profile for your training aircraft:

Pitch: _____

Power: _____

Maneuvering on the Water

Taxiing

There are three types of taxiing on the water: *idle taxi, step taxi,* and *plow taxi.*

Idle Taxi

Idle taxi is used to cover short distances on the water with good control and with minimal spray. Keep the stick full aft, unless you are idle taxiing downwind, in which case the stick will be full forward. Hold ailerons so that the wind is least likely to capsize the aircraft: "Climb into the wind; dive away from the wind" will help you remember the proper aileron position.

Use an idle power setting, such as 1000 RPM or less. (Increasing the power above this setting will *not* let you idle taxi faster; it will only bury the bows of the floats, creating an unstable and unsafe condition.)

Turning from downwind to upwind while idle taxiing is easy and safe; weathervaning assists you in the turn, so the turn will have a small radius.

Your ability to turn from upwind to downwind while idle taxiing will be limited by the wind speed, because now weathervaning is opposing your turn. If you are able to make this turn, the turn radius will be large. Again, resist the temptation to increase the power setting above 1000 RPM. If wind speed keeps you from making the turn from upwind to downwind, you will need to either use a plow taxi turn or sail downwind. Both are discussed later in this chapter.

Step Taxi

Step taxi is used to cover longer distances on the water for which idle taxi would be too slow, but which are too short to justify a takeoff and landing. Use a low cruise power setting, as described in "getting on the step" above. Hold (and trim) elevator pressure to maintain step taxiing pitch attitude of about 5° pitch up (or whatever pitch attitude your instructor recommends for your aircraft). When step taxiing straight ahead in a crosswind, hold ailerons into the wind (so that the wind is least likely to capsize the aircraft).

In a step taxi turn, always hold *full aileron in the direction of the turn*, regardless of the wind direction, again to minimize the risk of capsize.

A step taxi turn from upwind to downwind in a light-to-moderate breeze is feasible and safe. The aircraft is moving fast enough to overcome the weathervaning tendency, and the capsizing tendency from the wind is opposing the capsizing tendency from the turn itself.

A step taxi turn from downwind to upwind is dangerous (because the wind and the turn itself are both trying to capsize the aircraft) and should be avoided in anything more than a very light breeze.

Step taxi turns are summarized in the "Turning on the Water" section below.

Plow Taxi

Plow taxi is never used as a way to travel on the water (except that it is an unavoidable phase at the beginning of every water takeoff run). Its sole purpose is to allow a turn from upwind to downwind in a breeze too strong for an idle taxi turn. It is a busy, challenging maneuver that is only needed when the wind is strong, and even when done properly it exposes the propeller to spray damage, risks overheating the engine because of the high power setting with little cooling air flow, and exposes the aircraft to a significant risk of capsizing. The maneuver is summarized in Figure 5-5.

68 An Aviator's Field Guide to the **Seaplane Rating**

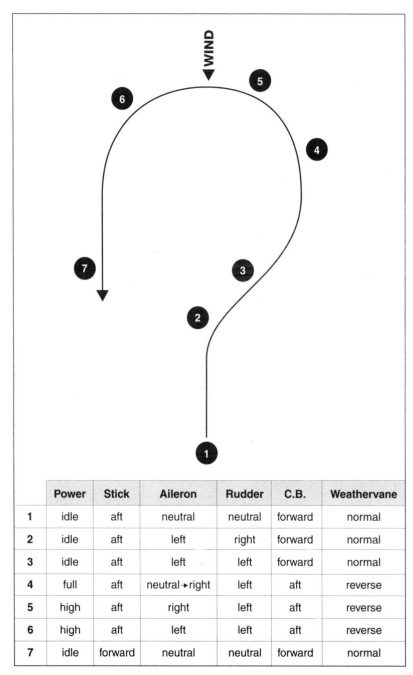

Figure 5-5. Plow taxi turn.

Chapter 5—Study Guide 69

* * *

Each type of taxiing on the water has its place. Every time you operate a seaplane, you will idle taxi—at least to maneuver from the dock to the start of your takeoff run, and to maneuver back to the dock or ramp after landing. You will step taxi as part of every water takeoff run, whenever you need to cover a distance on the water for which idle taxiing would just take too long, and after touchdown to quickly get closer to where you'll be docking. You may consider a plow taxi turn if you want to turn from upwind to downwind in a strong breeze, but in my view the disadvantages of a plow taxi turn outweigh the advantages, and sailing downwind (described later) is almost always the better option for moving from upwind to downwind in a strong breeze.

See Table 5-2 for a summary of the pros and cons of each type of taxiing on the water.

Table 5-2. Types of Taxiing on the Water

Types of taxiing	Pros	Cons
Idle	No spray; no overheating	Slow
Step	Fast; good cooling	Boat wakes; debris; porpoising
Plow	May allow turn downwind	Spray damage; poor cooling; risk of capsize

Turning on the Water

Plow Taxi Turn

For details of making a plow taxi turn, see Figure 5-5.

Turning While Idle Taxiing

- Downwind to upwind—Easy, safe, small radius; weathervaning is helping you turn.

- Upwind to downwind—Weathervaning is working against your turn. The radius of turn will be larger, and in a strong breeze the turn may not be possible due to weathervaning.

- *Resist the temptation to increase power to >1000 RPM: it will just bury the bows of the floats.*
- Other options:
  - Plow taxi.
  - Sail backward (almost always the better choice).

Turning While Step Taxiing

- Upwind to downwind—Safe, at least in light-moderate breeze, with a large radius.

- Downwind to upwind—UNSAFE: HIGH RISK OF CAPSIZE in more than a light breeze.

- For a smaller-radius step taxi turn, reduce power to the lowest setting that lets you remain on the step.

- *Note:* When you turn while step taxiing, even in no-wind conditions, a seaplane will have a tendency to tip, or even capsize, toward the outside of the turn. You must counteract this by holding **full aileron into the turn**: right aileron for a right step taxi turn, and left aileron for a left step taxi turn, regardless of the wind direction. This will help keep the outside wing up and the inside wing down.

- *Note:* In a step taxi turn, you usually need to increase power by an inch or two of manifold pressure to remain on the step and avoid porpoising.

A Note on Porpoising

Porpoising is an unstable bobbing of the nose up and down that tends to increase in amplitude. There is a real risk that in the "down" phase of the oscillation, the bows of the floats may dig into the water, causing pitchpoling and capsize.

Apart from oscillations caused by hitting boat wakes, porpoising is usually caused by a pitch attitude that is either too high or too low. Correcting a pitch attitude that is too high would require pitching down, which you don't want to do when porpoising because it may cause the bows to dig into the water. Therefore, choose the other option: pitch up in case you were at too low a pitch. If the porpoising then stops, carry on with the step taxi. But if it persists past two oscillations, *immediately* throttle back, come off the step, and start your step taxi over.

Taxiing Downwind

Idle Taxiing Downwind

Because of decreased airspeed (for example, if you are taxiing at 5 knots in a 5-knot tailwind, your airspeed is zero), your flight controls (including the air rudder) are less effective. This will result in decreased directional control, which could result in unintentional weathervaning. And in a strong tailwind, you must keep the control wheel forward so the wind will keep the tail down—otherwise the bows of the floats may bury.

Step Taxiing Downwind

To achieve a step taxiing airspeed of, for example, 40 knots in a 15-knot tailwind, your speed over the water will be 55 knots. This results in more drag on the floats than in a normal step taxi, and the resulting pitch down tendency could bury the bows of the floats, or forward movement of the center of buoyancy (CB) could result in a waterloop. In high winds, to go downwind, *sail instead.* (Sailing is discussed below.)

J-Turn for Takeoff in Confined Area

Step taxi downwind, then make a 180° step taxi turn upwind so that you're already on the step when you are headed into the wind, reducing the takeoff run.

Both parts of this maneuver are risky. The step taxi downwind is risky for the reasons discussed in the preceding section. The step taxi turn from downwind to upwind is risky because both the tipping tendency and the wind are working together to make the aircraft capsize to leeward, especially when you reach the point in the turn where the wind is abeam. For these reasons, you should *use this maneuver only if winds are light.* If winds are strong, you should have a short takeoff run anyway, so you won't need to make a J turn.

72 An Aviator's Field Guide to the **Seaplane Rating**

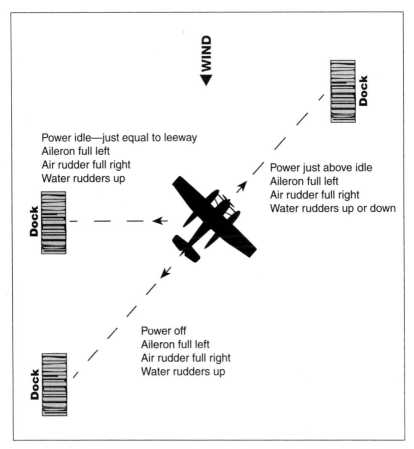

Figure 5-6. Sailing.

Sailing

Sailing is positioning the aircraft into the wind, with or without power, so as to maneuver on the water in controlled fashion in winds too strong to allow safe taxiing downwind (see Figure 5-6).

Sailing with power off:

- Water rudders up.
- Control wheel in the direction you want the aircraft to go.
- Air rudder opposite the control wheel (e.g., to sail to left, use left aileron and right rudder).

- The aircraft will sail backward in a path aligned with the keels of the floats, "toward the tail."

- In light breeze, you can increase the sailing speed by extending flaps/opening doors.

- In strong wind, you must use forward (down) elevator.

*Sailing with power **on**:*

- Water rudders up or down.

- Power at idle; adjust to hold position. (In light breeze, idle power will be too much to hold position, so power on sailing is only used in moderate or higher winds.)

- Air rudder in the direction you want to go.

- Control wheel opposite air rudder.

- If thrust just equals leeway, you will sail sideways in the direction toward which the nose is pointed, allowing you to "parallel park" if necessary.

Water Takeoffs

> *Note: For all takeoffs, determine in advance an abort point—a point by which you must be airborne. If not airborne by then, abort the takeoff. Make this part of your pre-takeoff briefing.*

Whenever possible, take off directly into the wind. If taking off from a canal or narrow river, this may not be possible; in this case, you will make a crosswind takeoff.

Current in the takeoff area (as you would encounter in a river or a tidal area) introduces a large number of variables. Considerations that may affect the decision of whether it is better to take off with the current (downstream) or against the current (upstream) include not only the speed of the current but also the speed and direction of the wind. Although a full discussion is beyond the scope of this course, further guidance is provided in Appendix C. General considerations include the following:

- Assuming wind is calm, you will get onto the step faster taking off upstream, but the takeoff run will be longer (because your speed relative to the water, and thus the drag of the floats on the water, will be greater when you're at flying airspeed).

- Taking off downstream, it will take a little longer to get on the step, but your takeoff run will be shorter.

- So, in general, *if wind is light, it's better to take off downstream.*

- However, it is much more complicated when there is more wind. There are lots of combinations, and no "one size fits all" rule, except that taking off downwind and into the current is the worst possible combination and should be avoided.

Normal Water Takeoff

- Get on the step as described for step taxi, except with 20° flaps.

- Keep power on full.

- At flying speed (about 50–55 KIAS in the Seabird), *don't rotate.* Maintain same pitch (5°–8° pitch up) and let it fly off.

- If it's not flying off and you have room, be patient but try increasing pitch up slightly.

- Alternatively, if you are running out of room, lift one float, and if you have turning room, don't try to maintain course with opposite rudder as this increases drag. (Less opposite rudder will be needed if you raise the left float than if you raise the right. Why? Because you are already having to use right rudder to overcome the left-turning tendencies due to P-factor, torque, rotating slipstream, and gyroscopic precession. If you raise the right float, you have to apply even more right rudder to counteract the added left-turning tendency from your left bank, and this large right rudder input further increases your drag. If you raise the left float by applying right aileron, instead of applying left rudder to counteract the right-turning tendency from your right bank, you can just reduce the right rudder you already have applied, so you reduce your drag.)

- Maintain same pitch (i.e., don't lose your pitch up attitude) while lifting a float.

- Lifting a float will result in a prompt takeoff.

- If not flying off despite having flying speed, another option is to "pop" the flaps momentarily to 40° (with thumb on the latch button on the end of the flap handle) then immediately back to 20°. Often, this will break you free.

Profile (pitch, power, attitude, and configuration) for a normal water takeoff in your training aircraft:

Flaps: _____

Pitch: _____

Power: _____

Attitude for step taxi: _____

Liftoff airspeed: _____

Crosswind Water Takeoff

There are three options for a crosswind water takeoff, and the first option is usually the easiest:

1. *Standard crosswind takeoff as if on land*—Aileron into the wind. Extend water rudders for directional control. After applying full throttle, immediately retract water rudders. Gradually decrease aileron input as airspeed increases.

2. *Planned weathervane*—Start takeoff run aiming for a point to leeward of the imaginary runway centerline on the water, knowing that the weathervaning tendency will veer you to windward.

3. *Downwind arc*—Start takeoff run diagonally into the wind, making an arcing step taxi turn away from the wind (so the capsizing tendency from the turn is opposed by the capsizing tendency of the wind), ideally lifting off approximately when wind is abeam.

Profile (pitch, power, attitude, and configuration) for a crosswind water takeoff in your training aircraft:

Flaps: _____

Pitch: _____

Power: _____

Attitude for step taxi: _____

Liftoff airspeed: _____

Glassy Water Takeoff

- The surface tension of smooth water keeps floats from breaking free of the water surface, increasing the takeoff run.

- Consider roughing up the surface by step taxiing in circles before beginning the takeoff run, to create ripples.

- When you have flying speed (50–55 knots in the Seabird), lift one float (left float preferred, but either will work). If you have room, allow the aircraft to turn gradually toward the side of the non-lifted float as you use aileron to lift the other float; maintaining a straight course with opposite rudder increases drag.

- Alternatively, you may try "popping the flaps" as described in the normal water takeoff section above.

- Obey your pre-briefed abort point.

- Glassy water makes it difficult to judge your height above the water, so after liftoff, you could inadvertently fly back into the water or pitch up too much and stall. Therefore, after liftoff,

Chapter 5—Study Guide   **77**

immediately go "on instruments," confirming and maintaining a positive rate of climb with the vertical speed indicator and proper pitch attitude with the attitude indicator.

Profile (pitch, power, attitude, and configuration) for a glassy water takeoff in your training aircraft:

Flaps: _____

Pitch: _____

Power: _____

Attitude for step taxi: _____

Liftoff airspeed: _____

Rough Water Takeoff

The height (crest to trough) and the wavelength (crest to crest) of the waves both matter. Waves more than one-tenth the length of your floats and/or more than one-half the depth of your floats may be too big. With the Seabird's twenty-foot-long floats, two-foot waves would be the absolute limit, and one-foot waves would still be rough water.

A short wavelength is better than a long wavelength: With a short wavelength, the floats can be supported on two crests, whereas with a long wavelength the floats can fall off one crest into a trough, digging the floats into the water with disastrous consequences.

Wave height is determined by wind speed and fetch. *Fetch* is the distance of open water the wind is blowing over. The longer the fetch, the higher the waves will be. With a north wind, for example, the waves will be higher at the south end of the lake than at the north end.

The *wavelength* is determined by the depth of the water (deeper water = longer wavelength) and by the direction of the water current relative to the direction of the wind. Wavelength will be longest if the wind is blowing the same direction as the current and will be shortest (i.e., the water will be choppiest) if the wind and current are in opposite directions.

Note that if the water is rough, the wind is almost certainly strong. This helps get you off the water more quickly, but until you get off, the pounding will be intense. To execute a rough water takeoff:

- Start with 40° of flaps, instead of the usual 20°.

- Position yourself directly into the wind.

- Wait until you are lifted on a crest to add full power.

- Maintain a slight pitch up attitude. If you use too much pitch up, the floats will slam into each crest; instead, you want to slice through them. Also, with too much pitch up you may stall if thrown into the air by a wave before you have flying airspeed. However, never allow the pitch to be so low that the bows of the floats dig into a wave.

- In contrast to a normal takeoff, in which you let the aircraft fly off the water without a definite rotation, in rough water you may be able to lift off sooner with a rotation as soon as you have flying speed (instead of just letting the aircraft fly off as you would normally do).

- Immediately after breaking free, accelerate in ground effect to V_X (65 knots in the Seabird), then climb out, raising flaps 10° at a time, taking care not to sink back onto the water surface.

Profile for a rough water takeoff in your training aircraft:

Flaps: _____

Pitch: _____

Power: _____

Attitude: _____

Rotation airspeed: _____

Confined Area Water Takeoff

There are at least two reasons a body of water may be considered "confined." First, the available distance to take off (or land) may be short. Second, rising terrain may make climbout impossible on the heading used for takeoff.

- In the case of a small lake/short available takeoff distance, you can try a J-shaped step taxi turn. The idea is to get on the step on a downwind heading, then while still on the step, make a 180° turn to windward to shorten the takeoff run. Note that this maneuver can be risky for two reasons. Step taxiing downwind can result in loss of yaw stability, a nose-over tendency, and the risk of a waterloop. And a step taxi turn from downwind to upwind may result in a capsize, as both the wind and "centrifugal force" tend to lift the upwind wing. For both of these reasons, *this maneuver should only be used if winds are light.*

- In even moderate winds, it is wise to consider limiting your windward step taxi turn to about 30°.

- Note that if winds are strong, you will likely be able to get off in a short distance anyway, without using this maneuver.

- If necessary to get off the water, lift one float (left float preferred) or "pop" the flaps.

- Once airborne, if confined by terrain, circle over the water while climbing to an altitude that lets you clear terrain, maintaining stall/spin awareness in the climb.

- Do not make your first turn after liftoff at less than your aircraft's minimum maneuvering speed (which is **not** the same as design maneuvering speed, V_A). This speed is 75 knots in the Seabird. This number will not be found in the AFM/POH; it is chosen to allow a safe margin over stall speed with a bank. *Ask your instructor what their preferred minimum maneuvering airspeed is in your training aircraft.*

Profile for a confined area water takeoff in your training aircraft:

Flaps: _____

Pitch: _____

Power: _____

Attitude for step taxi: _____

Liftoff airspeed: _____

Minimum maneuvering airspeed: _____

After Takeoff

For all types of takeoffs except rough water, and after accelerating to at least V_X in ground effect, follow the sequence in Table 5-3 for initial climbout.

Table 5-3. Initial Climbout Sequence

	Seabird 1850/1850A	Your training aircraft
1. Flaps	10°	
2. Initial climb airspeed (KIAS), until clear of obstacles straight ahead	$V_X = 65$	
3. Climb power	24"/2500	
4. Flaps	0°	
5. Climb airspeed	$V_Y = 75$	

Note: Even if your initial climb is at V_X to clear an obstacle, do not make your first turn on climbout at less than your "minimum maneuvering speed" (75 KIAS in the Seabird).

Chapter 5—Study Guide **81**

Water Landings

A water landing is done the same way in straight-float and amphibious seaplanes. But in preparation for landing—from pattern entry to short final—the amphib pilot must take care of some landing gear-related items that are not a concern for the straight-float pilot.

If you are training in a straight-float seaplane, my judgment is that studying procedures written for amphib pilots and trying to tune out the things that the amphib pilot must attend to complicates things unnecessarily. Therefore, I have chosen to present the preparation for water landings—from pattern entry until set up on final approach—in two versions: one for pilots training in straight-float aircraft, and one for pilots training in amphibs.

The following section first covers important considerations applicable to both straight-float and amphib seaplanes but then diverges into two parallel sections on setting up for water landings, which include the landing-gear related items in the amphib version and omits them in the straight-float version. You will use one section or the other, depending on which type of seaplane you're training in.

But once established on final, everything is once again the same for straight floats and amphibs, so the parallel sections will come together for the landing itself.

Preparing for Water Landing

Always assess the landing area before landing, as described in detail earlier in this chapter: Gather information before departure, and *always* fly over the intended landing area at 500 feet AGL to inspect it visually before landing.

Whenever possible, land directly into the wind. (This may be impossible in a canal or narrow river, in which case you will make a crosswind landing.)

Current in the landing area (as you would encounter in a river or a tidal area) introduces numerous variables. Considerations that may affect the decision of whether it is better to land with the current (downstream) or against the current (upstream) include not only the speed of the current but also the speed and direction of the wind, and whether you intend to dock upstream or downstream of your landing point. A full discussion is beyond the scope of this book, but in general:

- If wind is calm, landing with the current is preferable to landing against the current, because your speed relative to the water surface is lower and thus the drag of the water on the floats—and the forward pitching tendency—is less.

- If wind is strong and current is slight, landing into the wind is preferable, for the same reason.

- The worst possible combination is to land downwind and into the current.

- Regarding taxiing to the dock after landing: Again, there are many combinations, but be aware that you'll have least directional control taxiing downwind and downstream. This means that the best combination of wind and current for the landing itself may be less favorable, or even unfavorable, for taxiing to the dock.

Note:

- If you are flying a **straight-float seaplane**, continue with the "On Straight Floats" section below.

- If you are flying an **amphib seaplane**, skip to the "On Amphibious Floats" section on page 86.

On Straight Floats

Regardless of the type of landing you're making, *you must avoid two potentially disastrous errors:*

1. Landing in a crab and/or with sideways drift relative to the water surface.

2. Landing flat and fast.

Both of these errors can cause loss of directional control, and both may result in an accident.

For all landings, *determine an abort point:* a point (buoy, dock, tree, point of land, etc.) by which you will go around if you haven't touched down by then.

Normal water landing (see Figure 5-7):

- *Downwind:*
  - 500 feet AGL (= seaplane pattern altitude).
  - GUMPFARTS.
  - Throttle 20"/2500 RPM.
  - Flaps 0°.

- *Abeam touchdown point:*
  - Throttle 15", *then* prop full forward.
  - When in white arc, flaps to 20°.
  - Pitch and throttle for 75 KIAS. (Leave prop at 2500 RPM.)
  - Maintain 500 feet AGL.

- *Base:*
  - Maintain 500 feet AGL.
  - Flaps 20°.
  - Throttle to maintain 75 KIAS.

- *Final:*
  - Slight power reduction for 500 ft/min descent at 75 KIAS.

On the traffic pattern diagram in Figure 5-7, write in the corresponding profiles (pitch and power settings and resulting airspeeds) for your training aircraft at corresponding locations in the traffic pattern.

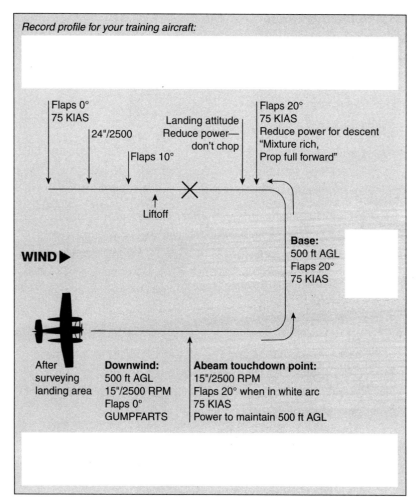

Figure 5-7. Traffic pattern for water landing/takeoff in straight-float seaplane.

Note: Now that you're established on final, skip to page 88 for a discussion of the landing itself, which as noted above will be the same for straight float and amphibious seaplanes.

On Amphibious Floats

Regardless of the type of landing you're making, *you must avoid three potentially fatal errors:*

1. Landing in a crab and/or with sideways drift relative to the water surface;

2. Landing flat and fast; and *especially*

3. Landing on the water with the gear down. The first two errors *may* result in an accident, but this one *always will*, and in one quarter of cases the accident is fatal.

For all landings, *determine an abort point:* a point (buoy, dock, tree, point of land, etc.) by which you will go around if you haven't touched down by then.

Normal water landing (see Figure 5-8):

- *Downwind:*
  - 500 feet AGL (= seaplane pattern altitude).
  - GUMPFARTS—The "U" for undercarriage means to make absolutely certain the **gear is UP** by all indicators: 2 blue lights, red tab in UP port in the deck of each float, visually (nose wheel), and if able, by mirror. Listen to the gear warning system's voice warning.
  - Throttle 20"/2500 RPM.
  - Flaps 0°.

- *Abeam touchdown point:*
  - Throttle 15", *then* prop full forward.
  - When in white arc, flaps to 20°.
  - Pitch and throttle for 75 KIAS. (Leave prop at 2500 RPM.)
  - Maintain 500 feet AGL.

- *Base:*
  - Maintain 500 feet AGL.
  - Flaps 20°.
  - Throttle to maintain 75 KIAS.
  - Recheck gear UP for water landing.

86 An Aviator's Field Guide to the **Seaplane Rating**

- *Final:*
  - Slight power reduction for 500 ft/min descent at 75 KIAS.
  - Check gear position by all indications again, then **SAY OUT LOUD**: "Mixture rich, prop full forward, gear is UP for water landing."

On the diagram in Figure 5-8, write in the profiles (pitch and power settings and resulting airspeeds) for your training aircraft at corresponding locations in the traffic pattern.

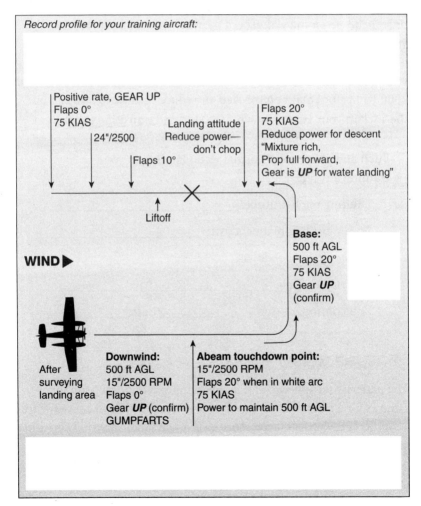

Figure 5-8. Traffic pattern for water landing/takeoff in amphib seaplane.

> **Note:** Now that you're established on final, the following sections cover the landing itself, which as noted above will be the same for straight float and amphibious seaplanes.

Normal Water Landing

When a few feet above water, transition to landing attitude, and gradually reduce power. Either keep a little power on until touchdown, or reduce power to idle if you're confident that you are only inches from the water, because when you reduce power to idle, you're going to come down fast. Either way, maintain pitch up about 8° until you settle on the water: your goal is to land on the steps of your floats. Immediately after touchdown, either add power (to about 2000 RPM) to remain on the step, or reduce throttle to idle and put the stick in your lap to come off the step and transition to idle taxi.

Pitch and power for a normal water landing in your training aircraft:

Landing pitch attitude: _____

Power just before touchdown: _____

Power after touchdown:

    If step taxiing: _____

    If coming off step: _____ idle _____

Crosswind Water Landing

The pattern and approach for a crosswind water landing are the same as for a normal landing. The absolute essentials in a crosswind landing on the water—even more so than on land—are that you must have no sideways drift and no crab when you touch down. Either, or both together, can result in a waterloop and a possible capsize. (See the FAA Safety Team video titled "Seaplane Safety—License to

Learn." [5] A lot of it is pretty disturbing, but the landing that pertains here occurs at about 1:59 from the beginning of the video.)

There are two options for crosswind landings:

1. Land just as you would on a runway, with aileron into the wind to eliminate sideways drift and opposite rudder to keep aligned with the "centerline." The problem is that there is no marked centerline to guide you, and on top of that, the apparent movement of the waves across your path will mislead you. With a left crosswind, for example, the waves appear to move from your left to your right. But the water is not moving left to right: A particle of water actually moves up and down (in a long, narrow vertical oval, actually) as a wave passes by; the water itself is not moving left to right. So if you try to land with no sideways motion relative to the waves, you will actually be landing drifting to the right relative to the water surface, with potentially disastrous consequences. On land, the centerline keeps you from doing this, but on the water, lacking a centerline, you must use a visual reference on shore—and ideally a "range" (two fixed objects that you can keep lined up relative to one another)—to prevent sideways drift. After touchdown, even if the dock you're going to is to windward, unless you immediately come off the step, you must turn downwind to reduce the risk of capsize from a step-taxi turn to windward.

2. Touch down when the wind is abeam, while you are in the middle of an arcing turn downwind. The idea is that at the moment of touchdown, the wind is trying to tip you to leeward, while the tipping tendency from your turn is trying to tip you to windward, so ideally the two cancel each other out. After touchdown, continue your downwind arc, and then come off the step. This option is trickier in my opinion, and I generally choose option 1.

---

[5] FAASTeam Safety Videos Archive, "Seaplane Safety—License to Learn," FAA Safety Team, Aug 30, 2012, YouTube video, 15:44, https://youtu.be/vBC0zVUAfFY.

Glassy Water Landing

This is the biggest surprise for most people learning to fly floats. Glassy water is beautiful and smooth, and it is reasonable to think that it would be the easiest water surface to land on. But in fact, it is perhaps the most dangerous, because it is impossible to judge accurately your height above smooth, glassy water. Because of this, you may either stall well above the water surface (thinking you are only inches above the water when in fact you may be 10 feet or more above the water) and drop onto the water, or you may fly the aircraft into the water surface thinking you still have plenty of altitude. Either could be disastrous. Landing close to shore will provide good visual reference and help you judge your height above the water, but when this is not possible (due to inadequate water depth or obstructions in the water, for example), here is what you do.

First, make sure you have plenty of landing distance available: I'd recommend at least three times your normal landing distance, because the glassy water approach will require much more distance than a normal approach.

Note that if the water is glassy, by definition the winds are very light, so you have your choice of landing direction. As you survey the lake to choose where you will cross the shoreline on your approach, if possible, choose a spot where the trees or terrain at the shoreline are low, so that you will have less altitude to lose on your approach (and thus your landing distance will not be as long).

Then set up a stabilized approach (see Figure 5-9). In the Seabird, I recommend flaps 20°, and while an argument can be made for a lower-than-normal airspeed, I recommend a normal approach airspeed of 75 KIAS. (If your training aircraft's POH/supplement makes a recommendation regarding glassy water airspeed, or if your instructor recommends a certain airspeed for your training aircraft, use that airspeed.) Your goal is to cross the shoreline just over the trees/terrain at the shore—which is your *last visual reference* (LVR)—at the lowest safe altitude above the trees/terrain, in landing pitch attitude (about 8° pitch up). Your descent rate will be normal until LVR. Then use power as needed to maintain 75 KIAS and a 100–150 feet per minute descent rate. (This is considerably more gradual than

90 An Aviator's Field Guide to the **Seaplane Rating**

your normal descent rate.) Hold this pitch and descent rate until you touch down; you may not feel it, and your only indication that you've touched down may be that you can see spray from the floats. Then pull throttle to idle, put the stick in your lap, and come off the step.

So: After arriving at LVR at 75 KIAS, flaps 20°, power 15"/2500 RPM (throttle as required), at a normal 300–500 feet per minute descent rate:

- Flaps 20°.
- Airspeed 75 KIAS.
- Power 17"/2500 RPM (throttle as required) to maintain 100–150 ft/min descent.
- Maintain this pitch/power until touchdown is confirmed.
- Power IDLE.
- Stick FULL AFT.
- Come off the step.

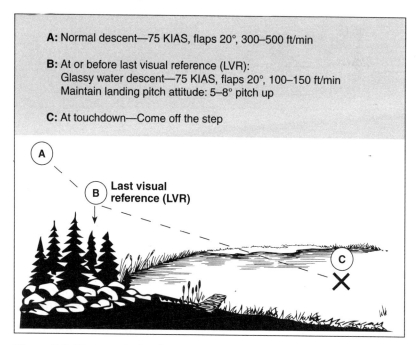

Figure 5-9. Glassy water landing.

For example, note that if your altitude above lake level at LVR was 150 feet, and your descent rate was 100 feet per minute after LVR, it would take one-and-a-half minutes until you touched down. At a ground speed of 75 knots, that would use up over two miles of lake! If your altitude at LVR was 100 feet above the water, you'll still use up a mile and a half. So as you can see, the lower you can be at LVR, the better—and it may be impossible to make a glassy water landing in a small lake.

Before beginning your approach to a glassy water landing, make your best effort to establish a go-around point: if you haven't touched down by that point, go around, because you have no way of knowing for sure how much more distance you're going to need before touchdown.

Profile (pitch, power, airspeed, and configuration) for a glassy water landing in your training aircraft:

Flaps: _____

Pitch: _____

Power: _____

Airspeed: _____

Rough Water Landing

Remember: "How rough is too rough?" depends on the wave height (crest to trough) and the wavelength (crest to crest) relative to the length of the floats. In the Seabird, one-foot waves are rough and two-foot waves are the absolute limit, and I would want a wavelength no greater than seven to ten feet. Your overall goal is to touch down with the step of the float on the crest of a wave, headed directly into the wind at minimum controllable airspeed, with a slight pitch up attitude (a little less pitch up than for a normal landing), with the keels of your floats slicing through the waves instead of slamming into them, and never allowing the bows to dig into a wave.

The approach is similar to a short-field landing on land: full flaps (instead of the normal 20°) and airspeed 70 knots (versus the normal 75 knots).

Unlike a short-field landing on land, for a rough water landing you will keep power on through the transition, so that at touchdown you're on the back side of the power curve, at minimum controllable airspeed.

After touchdown, come off the step immediately. Keep the stick in your lap to help minimize spray damage to the propeller and to help reduce the chance of the bows of the floats burying themselves in a wave.

To summarize, on short final:

- Flaps 40°.

- Airspeed 70 knots.

- Power 15"/2500 RPM (throttle as required to maintain airspeed).

- Touch down on a crest with slight pitch up (about 5–8°), power on, at minimum controllable airspeed.

- Immediately after touchdown:
  - Power to idle.
  - Stick full aft.

Profile (pitch, power, airspeed, and configuration) for a rough water landing in your training aircraft:

Flaps:_____

Pitch:_____

Power: _____(throttle as required)

Airspeed:_____, slowing to minimum controllable airspeed

Chapter 5—Study Guide 93

Confined Area Water Landing

This is in effect a short-field landing on the water. The approach is the same as for a rough water landing (or a short-field landing on land): full flaps (40°) and 70 knots. As you approach the water surface and transition to landing pitch attitude, you don't need to chop power to idle, but reduce it to idle more briskly than you would for a normal landing. There will not be much float at all. Make sure you maintain pitch up attitude (which will be harder with full flaps). After touchdown, come off the step immediately unless you know there are no obstructions between you and your dock/beach, and unless you are certain you have enough room to turn while on the step.

So, on short final:

- Flaps 40°.

- Airspeed 70 knots.

- Power 15"/2500 RPM (throttle as required to maintain airspeed and glide path to aiming point).

- Reduce power to idle in transition (beware—minimal float).

- Come off the step unless your path to dock/beach is clear.

Profile (pitch, power, and airspeed) for a confined area water landing in your training aircraft:

Flaps:_____

Pitch:_____

Power:_____, then idle just before touchdown

Airspeed:_____

Power-Off Emergency Landing

This is a general discussion of what to do if your seaplane's engine quits. These techniques will pertain to two ACS tasks: Emergency Approach and Landing (Simulated) and Power-Off 180° Accuracy Approach and Landing. (The former is required for all private ASES add-on candidates and for commercial candidates who hold AMEL without ASEL; the latter is required only for commercial candidates who hold AMEL without ASEL.) Your instructor will teach you the specifics of your required task(s).

As soon as you recognize that you have lost power, pitch down for best glide airspeed (for the Seabird, 85 KIAS clean) and *immediately* turn to your intended touchdown point, into the wind if possible. Unlike a power-off accuracy landing in a land plane, there really is no downwind leg in a power-off approach in a floatplane: When you lose power, you're coming down fast, which is why you turn immediately to your landing spot. It will require significant pitch down to maintain best glide speed with power off, and whereas in a normal landing you essentially fly the airplane down to the water in landing attitude, with power off you will need to transition fairly rapidly from this rather steep descent to a level—and then pitch up—attitude before you touch down. When you level off, you will lose speed rapidly: If you level off too high, you will stall and drop onto the water, so you need to level off just above the water surface and transition to landing attitude (about 8° pitch up). Hold your pitch up attitude until touchdown, and then keep the stick in your lap until you come off the step.

To summarize, *as soon as* you recognize power loss:

- Pitch for recommended glide speed (85 KIAS clean in the Seabird). The pitch down attitude will be impressive.

- Turn **immediately** toward your intended landing point; there is no downwind leg.

- Without power, prepare for **very** rapid decay of airspeed in the transition.
  - Flare too late—you'll slam into the water.
  - Flare too early—you'll stall and drop onto the water.

Chapter 5—Study Guide **95**

While flaps must be up to maximize your glide range and thus your chance of reaching water, the clean configuration results in a higher-than-normal landing speed. Ideally you would add flaps—ideally full flaps—after landing is assured, to reduce touchdown speed. However, you will find that things happen quite fast in a power-off landing in a seaplane, and if you are unable to add flaps while maintaining control of the aircraft, just make a flaps-up landing.

Your training aircraft's best glide speed, clean: _____

* * *

Regardless of the type of water landing you make, after landing on the water, you will either beach the aircraft, dock it, or taxi it up a ramp. These are detailed in the following sections.

Beaching

- *Preparation before departure*—Satellite photos; phone ahead for local knowledge.
- *Approaching the beach (assuming the breeze is generally blowing offshore—i.e., from the beach toward the water):*
  - Anchor/spare dock line ready.
  - Window open; door open.
  - Avionics master off; headset on glareshield, cord draped on map light so it won't snag you.
  - Master off.
  - Throttle idle (you can turn off one mag to reduce idle taxi speed).
  - Right hand on *mixture*, not on throttle, not on control wheel.
  - Approach at 45° so you can abort the approach if necessary.
  - Right foot for rudders, left foot on left float.
- *When about two float lengths away:*
  - Mixture full lean to shut down; mags off; coast in perpendicular to beach, steering with right foot.
  - Water rudders up when stopped.

96 An Aviator's Field Guide to the **Seaplane Rating**

- *When beached:*
  - Secure spare long dock line on aft cleat of leeward float; then while standing on shore, push bows off the beach and out to windward (weathervaning tendency will help you once the aircraft is afloat); pull stern in with dock line; this will spin the aircraft so the sterns of the floats are on the beach.
  - Secure dock lines from both stern cleats to two secure points of attachment on the shore: an anchor on the beach, a tree, etc.
  - Return to the flight deck to *double check* mags off, master off, seat belt not hanging out.

*Don't forget the option of sailing backward to the beach instead of nosing in. In a moderate or strong **onshore** breeze, this should be your first choice.*

Docking

- *Preparation before departure:*
  - Gather all the information you can about the dock you are planning to use. Look at it in Google Maps/Google Earth satellite photos. Call ahead and ask the owner about details, such as the piling height at low and high tide, obstructions such as a boathouse, etc. Ask the owner to send you photos of the dock, taken from the dock and, if possible, from the water as well. If possible, speak with a seaplane pilot who has used the dock.
  - Have fenders and a spare dock line readily available, so that you can tie them on quickly if needed after docking.

- *General principles of docking:*
  - As in boating, don't approach the dock any faster than you would want to crash into it—so ideally, you should plan your approach so that you're just coasting up to the dock at walking pace or less.
  - In general, assuming no current, you want to *dock in the direction that is most nearly into the wind*: The weathervaning tendency will help keep you aligned with the dock, you will

have good directional control, and when you shut down the engine, the wind will help you slow down. You will have none of these if you try to dock downwind, and in particular note that the weathervaning tendency will try to turn you around in the other direction.

Following is the normal docking approach (into the wind, with the wind blowing parallel to the dock and the dock on your left, and with minimal current. *Note: If the dock is on your right, you will need to slide over into the right seat and reverse the hand and foot instructions below):*

- Approaching the dock:
  - Window open; door open.
  - Avionics master off; headset on glareshield, cord draped on map light so it won't snag.
  - Master off.
  - Throttle idle (you can turn off one mag to reduce idle taxi speed).
  - Right hand on *mixture*, not on throttle, not on control wheel.
  - Approach at 45° so you can abort the approach if necessary.
  - Right foot for rudders, left foot on left float.

- When about two float lengths away:
  - Mixture full lean to shut down; mags off; coast in parallel to the dock, steering with right foot.
  - Water rudders up when stopped.

- When stopped at the dock:
  - Secure dock lines to float cleats fore and aft, and to cleats or other secure attachment point on the dock.
  - Put fenders between the floats and the dock and secure them to the aircraft or to the dock.
  - Return to flight deck to *double check* mags off, master off, seat belt not hanging out.

What if the wind is blowing onto the dock or off of the dock? You can still dock the seaplane, with adjustments. It is easier if the wind is blowing onto the dock: As you approach the dock at, for example, a 45° angle, the weathervaning tendency will tend to turn you parallel to the dock, and the wind will be blowing you toward the dock, so you can shut the engine down farther from the dock than normal—maybe three aircraft lengths.

If the wind is blowing off of the dock, you have two options. First, you can make a modified normal approach, approaching the dock at, say, 45°—but note that the wind is opposing your progress toward the dock, and the weathervaning tendency is opposing your turn to parallel the dock. Therefore, you'll need to delay engine shutdown until you are closer to the dock than you would be on a normal approach—maybe one aircraft length—so as to maintain directional control with water and air rudders, and to maintain forward progress toward the dock. The other option when the wind is blowing off the dock is to "nose up" to the dock—i.e., taxi up perpendicular to the dock. Be prepared to get out on the bow of a float (after making *certain* the mags are off) to fend off if necessary as you approach the dock, in case you were approaching too fast: The nose wheels of an amphib look like great bumpers, but hitting the dock too hard with the nose wheels will damage the struts, at great expense.

Figure 5-10. Power off, approaching the dock. *(iStock.com/shaunl)*

Runway Operations in an Amphibious Seaplane

In an amphib, *every runway takeoff is a soft-field takeoff, and every runway landing is a soft-field landing.*

Taxiing

There is no nosewheel steering on amphibious floatplanes: Steering is by braking only (except that the air rudder may be sufficient if taxiing with a headwind). To turn left, use the left brake. Tap the brakes, don't ride them: The brakes on many amphibs, the Seabird included, are undersized, and excessive braking will overheat the brakes and eat up brake pads.

Try to find the crown on the taxiway so that you don't have to keep braking to maintain a straight path. This means you may not be taxiing on the taxiway centerline; so be it. Slow down by reducing power well before you get where you're going so that you don't have to brake much to come to a stop or to enter a turn.

While taxiing, position the flight controls appropriately for the wind: "Climb into the wind; dive away from the wind." The center of gravity of a high-wing amphib on land is high, and the risk of being overturned in a strong wind is real.

Keep taxi speeds in the teens or less to minimize nosewheel shimmy. In calm or light winds keep the stick in your lap while taxiing, for the same reason.

Finally, note that on land, the pivot point for the aircraft is the main wheels, which are relatively aft (whereas on the water, the pivot point is the center of buoyancy, which at idle taxi is in the forward section of the floats). And recall that the nose wheels caster, so they offer essentially no resistance to turning. All of this means that on land, the aircraft will *reverse weathervane*—i.e., in a crosswind, it will head to leeward, just the opposite of what it does on the water.

Takeoff

- GUMPFARTS.

- Flaps 20°, full power, stick aft, like a soft-field takeoff. Your goal is to roll down the runway on the main wheels, with the nose wheels an inch or two off the runway.

- Then, just let it fly off whenever it flies off: There is no rotation. Pitch for V_X (65 KIAS in the Seabird) in ground effect and establish a climb at V_X.

- As soon as you are established in the climb, ***get the landing gear up***, even if you are remaining in the pattern. ("Positive rate, Gear UP.") ***Make this an unbreakable habit:*** If you always do this, you'll never land on the water with the gear down.

- Continue the V_X climb until clear of obstacles, then pitch for V_Y (75 KIAS in the Seabird).

- Reduce flaps to 10°, then reduce power to 24"/2500 RPM, then reduce flaps to 0°.

So, for a runway takeoff in the Seabird 1850A:

- Flaps 20°.

- Mixture best power.

- Prop full forward.

- Throttle full.

- Roll on mains, with nose wheels just off the ground.

- Let it fly off—no rotation.

- Pitch level, accelerate to V_X in ground effect.

- Climb at V_X.

- Positive rate of climb, gear up.

- Flaps 10°.

- Power 24"/2500 RPM climb power.

- Flaps 0°.

- Climb at V_Y when clear of obstacles.

A note on crosswind takeoffs on land: With a strong right crosswind, the reverse weathervaning tendency can be a real problem, because reverse weathervane is turning you to the left, as are all of the other factors—P-factor, torque, gyroscopic precession, and rotating slipstream—that affect any propeller-driven aircraft during takeoff. While you generally want your heels on the floor (i.e., no brakes) on the takeoff roll, with a strong right crosswind you may not be able to stay on the runway without using the right brake early in the takeoff roll. If the runway you are assigned for takeoff is going to give you a right crosswind component of 10 knots or more, you should request another runway if one is available. If another runway isn't available, and if the assigned runway is relatively wide, start the takeoff roll at the downwind edge of the runway, angled slightly to windward, to reduce the effective crosswind component.

Procedure and profile for a runway takeoff in your amphibious training aircraft:

_____

_____

_____

_____

_____

_____

_____

_____

Landing

- GUMPFARTS on downwind, including getting the gear down. Note that in many amphibious floats, including the Seabird's Mallard 3000A floats, the gear cycles quite slowly, so it is OK to get gear down before you're on downwind (i.e., before GUMPFARTS) so that you can confirm it's down before things get busy in the pattern.

- Power to 15" abeam the touchdown point; pitch up to maintain altitude (500 feet AGL).

- When in white arc (which will be almost immediately), flaps to 20° and power as needed to maintain 75 KIAS on base and final.

- Maintain 500 feet AGL until on final.

- On final, flaps to 30° and power as needed for a stabilized approach at 75 KIAS and 500 feet-per-minute descent.

- On final, check gear position visually again, then **SAY OUT LOUD**: *"Mixture rich, prop full forward, gear is DOWN for runway landing."*

- Over the threshold, round out, transitioning to landing attitude as you gradually reduce power. You can reduce power to idle only if you're pretty sure you are less than a foot above the runway, but in general it's best to treat it like a glassy water landing, or like a soft-field landing in a landplane: Keep a little power on as you descend gradually in landing attitude—there is not a flare—and touch down when you touch down.

- **You must touch down on the main gear**—no four-point landings, and heaven forbid, no landing nose wheels first (the nosewheel struts are breathtakingly expensive to repair or replace). This means you must have a definite pitch up attitude—about 8°, but you'll learn to eyeball it—when you touch down. If you are unsure whether you have enough pitch up, then pitch up more.

- After touchdown, put the stick in your lap to reduce the nosewheel shimmying tendency.

Profile for a normal runway landing in your amphibious training aircraft:

Flaps on final approach: _____

Airspeed on final approach: _____

Chapter 6
Oral Exam Preparation Questions

ACS codes are provided after each of the questions in this chapter to identify the relevant ACS tasks that they address. ACS codes beginning with "PA" are from the *Private Pilot for Airplane Category Airman Certification Standards* (FAA-S-ACS-6), and codes beginning with "CA" are from the *Commercial Pilot for Airplane Category Airman Certification Standards* (FAA-S-ACS-7). Full ACS codes include four components identifying the elements within each task. For example, PA.I.F.K2:

PA = Applicable ACS

I = Area of Operation

F = Task

K2 = Task element (in this example, Knowledge 2)

This chapter includes only the first three components (applicable ACS, area of operation, and task; for example, PA.I.F) in each ACS code to identify the tasks that apply to each question.

105

Questions

(Answers are provided beginning on page 121.)

1. Using the airplane flight manual (AFM)/pilot's operating handbook (POH) and float supplement for your training aircraft, find as many of the following as you can for your aircraft.

	Your training aircraft
Maximum gross weight (lb)	
Useful load (lb)	
Full fuel payload (lb)	
Takeoff distance (50 ft obstacle) (ft) @max gross, sea level, std temp, zero wind, normal takeoff flaps:	
On water	
On land (*amphib only*)	AMPHIB
Landing distance (50 ft obstacle) (ft) at max gross weight, sea level, standard temp, zero wind:	
On water (flaps _____)	
On land (flaps _____) (*amphib only*)	AMPHIB
Fuel capacity (gallons) (usable)	
Fuel type	
Oil capacity (qt)	
Minimum oil	
Engine model/HP	
Approx. cruise fuel consumption (gph)	
Minimum hangar door height (ft)	
Minimum maneuvering airspeed (KIAS)	
Best glide airspeed (KIAS)	
Max RPM for idle taxi	

[PA.I.F; CA.I.F]

2. In your training aircraft, you have 25 gallons of fuel on board. Your examiner weighs 200 pounds, and it's only you and the examiner on board for your checkride today. Using your actual weight, is your training aircraft within weight and balance limits?

   Total weight: _____ Within limits?_____

   Total moment: _____

   C.G.: _____ Within limits? _____

   [PA.I.F; CA.I.F]

3. Your passenger needs to land for an emergency bathroom break while flying through unfamiliar territory. There is a lake nearby, but you are not sure whether it is long enough for you to land on and take off from. How can you determine the length of the lake without the use of an electronic device like a tablet or phone?

   [PA.I.F, PA.II.B; CA.I.F, CA.II.B]

4. You are taking off from a relatively small lake with trees lining the north shore. A nearby ATIS is reporting wind 360° at 8 knots. In the following aircraft, what airspeed will you accelerate to in ground effect and then climb out at, and why?

   a. In the Seabird 1850/1850A?

   b. In your training aircraft?

   [PA.I.F; CA.I.F]

5. Your engine has just failed. What speed will you pitch for and maintain in the descent, and why?

   a. In the Seabird 1850/1850A?

   b. In your training aircraft?

   [PA.I.F; CA.I.F, CA.IX.C]

6. Describe the path of fuel to the cylinders after engine start in your training aircraft.

   [PA.I.G; CA.I.G]

Chapter 6—Oral Exam Preparation Questions **107**

7. How (manually, electrically, hydraulically) are the following controlled in your training aircraft?

    a. Flaps: _____

    b. Air rudder, elevator, ailerons: _____

    c. Water rudders: _____

    d. Landing gear (*amphib only*): _____

    [PA.I.G; CA.I.G]

8. In the event of a complete electrical failure (alternator/ battery) in your training aircraft, list the systems and items that would become inoperative and the systems and items that would continue to function.

    [PA.I.G; CA.I.G, CA.IX.C]

9. In the Seabird 1850/1850A, if the propeller governor lost oil pressure, the propeller would go to low pitch/high RPM, which would add the drag of a windmilling propeller to the high drag of the aircraft itself—making a bad situation (loss of power) worse.

    In your training aircraft (if equipped with a constant-speed propeller), what would occur with a loss of oil pressure in the propeller governor?

    [PA.I.G; CA.I.G, CA.IX.C]

10. (*Amphib only*) In the Seabird 1850A there are five indicators of landing gear position:

    - Blue (gear up) or amber (gear down) gear position indicator lights on the panel.

    - A red flag on the top of the float visually indicates gear position.

    - A mirror on the strut lets you see the position of the main gear on the opposite float.

    - From the flight deck, you can see the position of the nose gear on the opposite float.

- The landing gear warning system (annunciator and voice warning) indicates gear position.

  If you are flying an amphibious training aircraft, what indicators of landing gear position does it have, and how will you avoid landing on the water with the gear down?

  [PA.I.G; CA.I.G]

AMPHIB

11. What three mistakes (one of them an issue only for amphibs, the other two applicable to all seaplanes) can you never afford to make while landing a seaplane on the water, and what are the consequences of each?

    [PA.I.G; CA.I.G]

12. If a seaplane's floats are rated at 3,000 pounds and the aircraft's maximum gross weight is 3,300 pounds, will the seaplane sink? Why or why not?

    [PA.I.G, PA.I.I; CA.I.G, CA.I.I]

13. Name the following parts of a seaplane float:

    a. The part you stand and walk on: _____

    b. The entire structure that is submerged: _____

    c. The last part that leaves the water when you take off, and the first part that touches water when you land. (It is also the strongest part.): _____

    d. Reinforced member that runs from the bow to the aft end of the step: _____

    e. Separates one compartment from the next: _____

    f. The part you tie a dock line to: _____

    g. Stout streamlined bars, one forward and one aft, running laterally from one float to the other: _____

    h. Reduces water spray damage to propeller: _____

    i. Joins the vertical side of the float to the keel: _____

    j. Allows directional control when idle taxiing: _____

    [PA.I.I; CA.I.I]

Chapter 6—Oral Exam Preparation Questions 109

14. What is the center of buoyancy of a seaplane float, and why does it matter?

[PA.I.I; CA.I.I]

15. You are idle taxiing on a lake, preparing for takeoff. There are no flags or smokestacks visible and no nearby ATIS, and from the surface, you can't be sure of the orientation of ripples on the water surface. How can you determine the direction of the wind? Explain how this method works.

[PA.I.I; CA.I.I]

16. You are flying over a lake in a forest to inspect the lake before landing. You notice ripples that are oriented north–south and that cover the entire lake except the eastern shore, where the water is glassy. You do not see streaks. What can you say, if anything, about the speed and/or direction of the wind?

[PA.I.I; CA.I.I]

17. You are idle taxiing westward toward a dock that is oriented north–south. A nearby airport's ATIS reports wind 360 at 4 knots. When you are 30 feet from the dock, you realize that you are going too fast.

    a. What will happen if you apply the brakes, as you would do in a land plane?

    b. How can you avoid crashing into the dock?

    [PA.I.I, PA.XII.B; CA.I.I, CA.XI.B]

18. How can you identify a seaplane base

    a. on a sectional chart?

    b. from the air at night?

    [PA.I.I; CA.I.I]

19. How can you find out whether you can legally land on a specific body of water?

    [PA.I.I; CA.I.I]

110 An Aviator's Field Guide to the **Seaplane Rating**

20. Why is 14 CFR §91.115 pertinent to seaplane pilots?

    [PA.I.I; CA.I.I]

21. You are idle taxiing northward on a lake. Ahead and to your right, you see a boat proceeding slowly westward. It appears that your seaplane and the boat will collide unless one of you changes course/speed. Who should change their course/speed? Why?

    [PA.I.I; CA.I.I]

22. While you are step taxiing, a speedboat comes out of nowhere and looks like it is going to crash into you. Who has the right-of-way?

    [PA.I.I; CA.I.I]

23. If you are taking off or landing on a lake and there are boats already on the lake, who has the right-of-way?

    [PA.I.I; CA.I.I]

24. You are idle taxiing. Who has the right-of-way between you and each of the following, if it appears you will collide?

    i. A massive container ship

    ii. A 12-foot sailboat with no motor

    iii. A personal watercraft (Jet Ski)

    [PA.I.I; CA.I.I]

25. Is there *any* situation in which you in a seaplane would unequivocally have the right-of-way over a boat on the water?

    [PA.I.I; CA.I.I]

26. You are taxiing upstream in a river with standard navigational markers. You notice a green buoy on your left.

    a. Are you in the channel?

    b. Do those markers even pertain to you (piloting a seaplane)?

    [PA.I.I; CA.I.I]

Chapter 6—Oral Exam Preparation Questions **111**

27. You are taxiing southward in the Intracoastal Waterway along the South Carolina coast. On your right, you notice a wooden pole with a triangular red sign with a number on it. Are you in the channel?

[PA.I.I; CA.I.I]

28. You are on final approach to the only good landing area on a lake, and you notice another seaplane on its takeoff run on the same "runway." What is your response?

[PA.I.I; CA.I.I]

29. What four risk elements does the FAA require pilots to consider before every flight, regardless of the type of aircraft?

[PA.II.A; CA.II.A]

30. What does 14 CFR §91.103(b) require pilots to know before every flight, regardless of the type of aircraft?

[PA.II.A; CA.II.A]

31. How does the preflight inspection of a seaplane differ from the preflight inspection of a land plane?

[PA.II.A; CA.II.A]

32. While pumping out a float compartment during your preflight inspection, you get no water at all, and there is really no resistance to the pump. Maybe there is just no water at all in that compartment (it can happen). However, what else may be going on?

[PA.II.A; CA.II.A, CA.IX.C]

33. *(Amphib only)* You flew late yesterday afternoon, and it rained overnight. You have a flight scheduled this morning, and you're running late. It is kind of a pain to pump out the float compartments, so you are considering skipping that step just this once. Is there any downside to doing this?

[PA.II.A; CA.II.A]

112 An Aviator's Field Guide to the **Seaplane Rating**

34. You are flying single pilot today and have two passengers on board the aircraft—one in the copilot's seat and one in the second row. How will you brief your passengers for this flight, and how will you silently brief yourself for this takeoff and departure?

[PA.II.B; CA.II.B]

35. In your training aircraft as equipped, could you legally

a. enter Class C airspace?

b. do an LPV approach?

[PA.II.B; CA.II.B]

36. Fill in the details in the table below for idle taxiing and step taxiing in your training aircraft.

	Your training aircraft	
	Idle taxi	Step taxi
Throttle		
Prop (if applicable)		
Flaps		
Stick position*		
Pitch		
Water rudders (up/down)		
Weathervaning tendency (normal/reverse)		

*Exception: when idle taxiing downwind, the stick must be full forward.

[PA.II.E; CA.II.E]

37. You are idle taxiing on a lake. Before landing, you noticed wave crests running east–west, streaks running north–south, a few whitecaps, and a band of calm water along the north shore. Describe what will happen in the following situations.

a. While taxiing southward, you turn to the north.

b. While taxiing northward, you attempt to turn to the south.

[PA.II.E; CA.II.E]

Chapter 6—Oral Exam Preparation Questions 113

38. You are step taxiing on a lake. Before landing, you noticed wave crests running east–west, streaks running north–south, a band of calm water along the north shore, and no whitecaps.

   a. While taxiing northward, is it safe to turn to the south? Explain why or why not, and any precautions that you should consider.

   b. While taxiing southward, is it safe to turn to the north? Why or why not?

   [PA.II.E; CA.II.E]

39. While step taxiing, you begin porpoising.

   a. What should you do immediately?

   b. If the porpoising does not stop after two oscillations, what should you do, and why?

   [PA.II.E; CA.II.E]

40. Under what circumstances might you *consider* making a plow taxi turn?

   [PA.II.E; CA.II.E]

41. Once you finish your training, why will you never actually do a plow taxi turn?

   [PA.II.E; CA.II.E]

42. Because of lowering cloud ceilings, you have landed on a 2,500-foot-diameter lake and have beached on the north shore. Now the ceilings have improved. What options would you consider for positioning yourself to begin the takeoff run if the wind is

   a. from the north at 5 knots?

   b. from the north at 15 knots?

   [PA.II.E; CA.II.E]

43. You are docked on a lake. The wind is from the north at 15 knots. You need to move your seaplane to a dock 100 yards southeast of your current dock for fuel. You wisely decide against a plow taxi turn and choose to sail instead. How will you position your flight controls and water rudders to sail to your new dock?

[PA.II.E; CA.II.E]

44. a. What does each letter in the GUMPFARTS before-takeoff checklist flow represent?

G _____

U _____

M _____

P _____

F _____

A _____

R _____

T _____

S _____

b. If your instructor uses a different before-takeoff checklist flow for your training aircraft, enter it below, including what each letter of their flow represents.

_____

_____

_____

_____

_____

_____

[PA.II.F; CA.II.F]

45. You have flown over the lake you intend to land on, and you have determined that the landing area is long enough for today's conditions, that the wind and water surface are within your and your aircraft's capabilities, and that there are no sandbars, logs, or other obstructions in your intended landing area. You are now positioning yourself for landing. Refer to the traffic pattern diagram shown in Figure 6-1, and for each position indicated by a letter, fill in the applicable information in the table below.

[PA.III.B; CA.III.B]

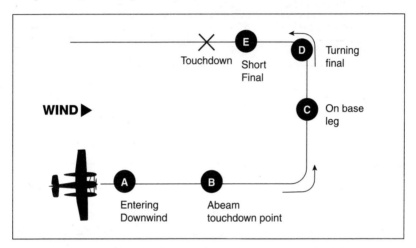

Figure 6-1. Traffic pattern diagram.

	Your training aircraft					
	A	**B**	**C**	**D**	**E**
Altitude (AGL)					
Throttle/prop (RPM)					
Flaps					
Gear (amphib)					
Airspeed (KIAS)					
Checklist/flow					

46. You are on a large lake, and the surface has ripples but no streaks. You have idle taxied your training aircraft to your intended takeoff point and have pointed the aircraft to windward. Having completed your before takeoff checklist/flow, you pull the stick into your lap and apply full power.

    a. How do you counteract left-turning tendencies at the beginning of the takeoff run?

    b. How do you maintain directional control once you've gotten on the step?

    c. How do you know when it is time to lift off?

    d. What are your options if you have reached flying speed and you are not lifting off?

    e. After accelerating in ground effect, at what speed will you climb out if there are no obstacles in your path?

    [PA.IV.A; CA.IV.A]

47. You are taking off from a narrow lake in a floatplane. There is a direct 12-knot crosswind. You can choose to take off with a right crosswind or a left crosswind. Does it matter which you choose? Why or why not?

    [PA.IV.A; CA.IV.A]

48. (*Amphib only*) You are taking off from the single runway at a nontowered field in an amphibious floatplane. There is a direct 12-knot crosswind. You can choose to take off with a right crosswind or a left crosswind. Does it matter which you choose? Why or why not?

    [PA.IV.A; CA.IV.A]

    AMPHIB

49. You are landing to the west in a 100-yard-wide river that runs east–west. Wind is from the north at 12 knots. There happens to be a piling (tall post) near the middle of the river, a mile beyond where you intend to land, and there is a tall tree on shore half a mile beyond the piling.

(continued)

Chapter 6—Oral Exam Preparation Questions   **117**

How will you avoid touching down while drifting sideways?

[PA.IV.B; CA.IV.B]

50. The ForeFlight measuring tool you used in your pre-departure trip planning showed that the circular lake you have just landed on is only 3,000 feet in diameter. Because you used Google Earth, backed up by a topographic map, you knew in advance that there was high terrain on all sides. Landing wasn't too much of a problem because of a gap in the terrain, but now it's time to take off, and that gap in the terrain is downwind. Before landing a few minutes ago, you noted ripples but no streaks on the water surface.

    a. How will this takeoff differ from a normal takeoff?

    b. If you don't lift off promptly upon reaching flying speed, what will you do?

    c. How are you going to get out of there, given that you can't outclimb the terrain straight ahead?

[PA.IV.G; CA.IV.G]

51. Your destination is yet another small lake, this time with terrain on all sides. How will this approach and landing differ from a normal approach and landing in your training aircraft?

[PA.IV.H; CA.IV.H]

52. Your destination is your friend's dock at the south end of a large lake. Your friend's house is surrounded by a stand of 50-foot-high trees, which are the only trees on the entire shoreline. When you fly over the lake to inspect it before landing, the wind appears to be calm, and you see no ripples and no streaks on the water surface. Describe your final approach and landing in this scenario and any concerns you have.

[PA.IV.I; CA.IV.I]

53. You are departing a friend's dock at the south end of a large lake. Your friend's house is surrounded by a stand of 50-foot-high trees, which are the only trees on the entire shoreline. The wind

seems to be calm, with no ripples and no streaks visible on the water surface.

a. Will the stillness of the water make it easier or harder to get airborne? Why?

b. What can you do (before and during the takeoff run) to help break free of the water surface?

c. How can you keep from flying back into the water surface, or from pitching up too high and stalling, just after liftoff?

[PA.IV.J; CA.IV.J]

54. You are departing a friend's dock at the south end of a large lake. Your friend's house is surrounded by a stand of 50-foot-high trees, which are the only trees on the entire shoreline. Wave crests on the lake run east–west, and there are north–south streaks with numerous whitecaps. The marine weather report states seas are 1–2 feet. How will you take off in these conditions?

[PA.IV.K; CA.IV.K]

55. After departing from your friend's lake dock, you are halfway home when you realize that you left your phone and need to return to retrieve it. You return to the lake, arriving an hour after you had left. You still see lots of streaks on the lake, but now far fewer whitecaps than when you departed. You see small waves breaking on the beach. How will this approach and landing differ from normal?

[PA.IV.L; CA.IV.L]

56. Your flaps are stuck in the up position. You are lined up on final approach, but you are high. Describe how to lose altitude without increasing your airspeed.

[PA.IV.M; CA.IX.C]

57. The unpopulated lake you have just inspected from 500 feet AGL has ripples and streaks but few, if any, whitecaps. On downwind, abeam your intended touchdown point, which is adjacent to the only dock on the lake, your engine fails. Because you will

not be able to taxi (other than sailing, which is slow) after touchdown, and you are not a strong swimmer, you would like to touch down as close to the dock as possible. Describe how you will try to accomplish that.

[PA.IX.B; CA.IV.M (*multi-engine only*), CA.IX.B]

58. You are passing over the airport of a medium-sized coastal (sea level) city, enroute in an amphib seaplane at 6,000 feet to your destination an hour away, when your passenger develops chest pain and thinks he is having a heart attack. You declare an emergency and request EMS. You need to get your passenger on the ground. How will you get to pattern altitude as quickly as possible?

[PA.IX.A]

59. You are docked on the east side of a long dock that runs north–south. Your aircraft is pointed northward. What challenges will you encounter as you try to leave the dock with the wind from the east? With the wind from the west?

[PA.XII.B; CA.XI.B]

60. You are arriving at a long dock that runs north–south. Wind is from the northeast. While there are several options, you choose to dock along the east side of the dock, headed north. Describe your approach to the dock.

[PA.XII.B; CA.XI.B]

61. Your destination is your small private island in the center of a large lake. Your island is rocky, except for a beach along the north shore. You have landed directly north of the island. Before landing, you noticed ripples running east–west, streaks running north–south, a few whitecaps, and glassy water along the south shore of the island. How will you get to your beach?

[PA.XII.B; CA.XI.B]

Answers

1. *Answers will vary depending on your training aircraft. Refer to the information in the airplane flight manual (AFM) pilot's operating handbook (POH) and float supplement for your aircraft.*

   As an example, data for the Seabird 1850/1850A is shown below:

	Seabird 1850/1850A
Maximum gross weight (lb)	3300
Useful load (lb)	1000/900
Full fuel payload (lb)	634/534
Takeoff distance (50 ft obstacle) (ft) @ max gross, sea level, std temp, zero wind, normal takeoff flaps:	
On water	1400/1600
On land (*amphib only*)	Not applicable/1400
Landing distance (50 ft obstacle) (ft) at max gross weight, sea level, standard temp, zero wind:	
On water (flaps _____)	2000
On land (flaps _____) (*amphib only*)	Not applicable/1600
Fuel capacity (gallons) (usable)	61
Fuel type	100LL
Oil capacity (qt)	12
Minimum oil	8, prefer 9
Engine model/HP	"IO300," 285
Approx. cruise fuel consumption (gph)	17
Minimum hangar door height (ft)	13
Minimum maneuvering airspeed (KIAS)	75
Best glide airspeed (KIAS)	85
Max RPM for idle taxi	1000

2. *Answers will vary. Refer to the information on your training aircraft's weight and balance data/envelope in the airplane flight manual (AFM)/pilot's operating handbook (POH) and float supplement.*

3. Measure the time required to cross the lake at a known speed. Then multiply the time in seconds by your speed in feet per second to find the distance in feet. For example, if it takes you 24 seconds to cross the lake at 100 knots, you would calculate the lake length as follows:

    100 kt is 169 ft/sec

    So: 24 sec × 169 ft/sec = 4,056 feet

4. a. In the Seabird 1850/1850A: You will climb at V_X (to clear the trees) = 65 KIAS.

    b. To clear the trees, you will climb at V_X, which in your training aircraft is _____ KIAS. (*Refer to AFM/POH.*)

5. a. In the Seabird 1850/1850A: 85 KIAS = best glide speed.

    b. You will pitch for and maintain best glide speed V_G, which in your training aircraft is _____ KIAS. (*Refer to AFM/POH.*)

6. *Refer to the fuel system schematic in your training aircraft's AFM/ POH. An answer is provided below for the example Seabird 1850/1850A (see Figure 6-2):* In the Seabird 1850/1850A, which has high wings, fuel is fed from each wing tank to the engine by gravity, via a fuel tank selector/shut-off valve, assisted when needed by an electric boost pump. After engine start, the engine-driven fuel pump pumps fuel to a fuel control unit, controlled by mechanical inputs from the throttle and mixture control, to a distributor, from which proceed six fuel lines, one for each cylinder. Each line terminates with a fuel injector, which sprays fuel into the intake manifold just outside the combustion chamber of that particular cylinder.

7. *Refer to your training aircraft's AFM/POH. As an example, answers are provided below for the Seabird 1850/1850A:*

    a. Flaps—Mechanically

    b. Air rudder, elevator, ailerons—Mechanically

    c. Water rudders—Mechanically

    d. Landing gear (amphib only)—Electrically activated, hydraulically actuated (see Figure 6-3)

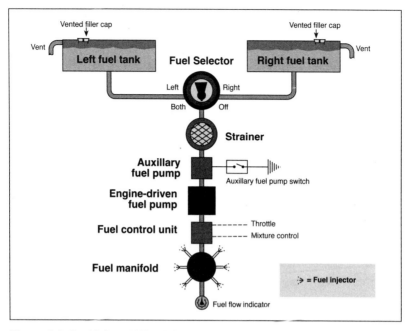

Figure 6-2. Seabird 1850/1850A fuel system schematic.

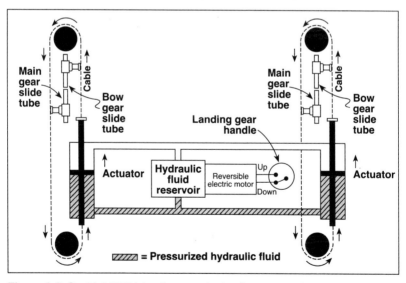

Figure 6-3. Seabird 1850A landing gear hydraulic system schematic. (Automatic only: hand pump system not shown.)

8. *Refer to your training aircraft's electrical system schematic in the AFM/POH. As an example, an answer is provided below for the Seabird 1850/1850A (See Figures 6-4 and 6-5):* If the alternator were to fail and the battery were to go completely dead in the Seabird 1850/1850A, the engine would work perfectly normally, as would the ailerons, elevator, rudder (air and water), flaps, pitot-static instruments, and vacuum instruments. The turn coordinator, interior and exterior lights, radios, VOR's GPS, and transponder (including ADS-B) would not work. In the 1850A, the gear position handle would not change the gear position, and the gear advisory system would not work, but the gear could be raised and lowered with the manual pump, and the mechanical/visual means of assessing gear position would still be available.

9. Verify with your aircraft's POH/AFM. In almost all single-engine aircraft with constant-speed propellers, loss of oil pressure to the propeller governor causes the propeller to revert to a low pitch/high RPM/high windmilling drag position (in contrast to most twins, which revert to a low-drag feathered position).

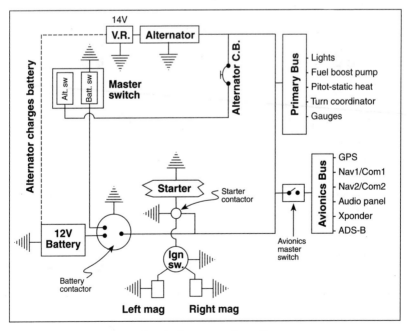

Figure 6-4. Seabird 1850 electrical system schematic.

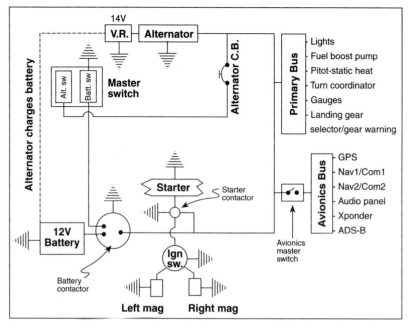

Figure 6-5. Seabird 1850A electrical system schematic.

10. *Refer to the POH/AFM for the landing gear position indicators in your aircraft.*

    There are multiple procedures to ensure you avoid landing on the water with the gear down. First, you will develop the unbreakable habit of raising the gear immediately after every takeoff, as soon as you are climbing ("Positive rate, GEAR UP"), even if you are doing laps in the pattern. Second, you will complete GUMPFARTS (or your instructor's preferred flow) on downwind. Third, you will verify gear position on base and again by all indicators on final approach, and having done so, will say *out loud*, "Mixture rich, prop full forward, GEAR IS UP FOR WATER LANDING."

11. Mistakes while landing a seaplane on the water:

   a. Touching down while drifting sideways, which may result in loss of directional control, possible collision, or capsize.

   b. Landing flat and fast: When you land on the forward portion of the float instead of on the step, the center of buoyancy, which is the pivot point, is too far forward. In particular, it is forward of the center of gravity, just like a tailwheel aircraft on land. And just like a tailwheel aircraft on land, the seaplane is now directionally unstable. When you land fast, there is more frictional drag than normal on the floats. This causes a forward tipping moment, moving the center of buoyancy even farther forward and further reducing directional control. All of this can lead to a collision or capsize.

   c. *Amphibs only*: Landing on the water with landing gear down. This typically results in *pitchpoling*, meaning that the aircraft flips end over end and comes to rest inverted. Occupants are at best stunned and disoriented, and at worst unconscious from impact. Egress is difficult at best and may be impossible.

12. 3,000 lb ÷ 0.9 = 3,333 lb. This is the maximum gross weight of an aircraft that can be supported by floats rated at 3,000 pounds. Therefore, the seaplane is certainly not overfloated, but it is within limits.

13. a. Deck

   b. Hull

   c. Step

   d. Keel

   e. Bulkhead

   f. Cleat

   g. Spreaders

   h. Spray rail

   i. Chine

   j. Water rudders

14. The center of buoyancy (CB) is the point about which the aircraft pivots while on the water. When idle taxiing (or anchored or moored) the CB is forward, and the structures that the wind strikes, such as the vertical stabilizer, are well aft, so the aircraft *weathervanes* to point into the wind. This is referred to as normal weathervaning. In a plow taxi turn (or before you get on the step at the beginning of the takeoff run) the CB is well aft, and there is more to catch the wind forward of the CB, so the aircraft will *reverse weathervane*—a much less stable situation.

15. Retract the water rudders. In an idle taxi, you will weathervane (normal, not reverse). When the oscillations settle down, you will be pointed directly into the wind.

16. Ripples are always perpendicular to the wind. North–south ripples mean the wind is either from the east or the west. Ripples without streaks means the wind is in the 3–7 knot range. The glassy eastern shore means that the wind is from the east.

17. a. Nothing, because seaplanes on the water have no brakes.

   b. Long before you are 30 feet from the dock, you could have gone from both magnetos to left or right magneto only, to reduce power while still idling. At this point, pull mixture to idle cut-off, turn ignition off, take headset off, open the left door, put your left foot out while steering the water rudders with your right foot, and begin a turn to the right to come alongside the dock heading north (into the wind, so the wind will help slow you down).

18. a. Refer to the sectional chart legend. A seaplane base is marked with an anchor (the shank of which indicates the preferred takeoff/landing direction).

   b. A seaplane beacon is yellow and white, not green and white.

19. To determine whether you can legally land on a specific body of water:

    - Navigable waterways, including the Intracoastal Waterway, are generally open to seaplanes.

    - The Seaplane Pilots Association's Water Landing Directory app lists most lakes and other waterways by state, and indicates whether the body of water is open (including any restrictions), closed, or unknown.

    - If the status of the waterway is unknown, then you must find out who the governing agency is (it could be a municipality, the state's Department of Natural Resources, a Sheriff's Department, etc.) and seek that agency's permission. If you are trying to get a controlling agency to open a waterway to seaplane operations, get the Seaplane Pilots Association involved; they have a better chance than you or me alone of opening those doors.

20. 14 CFR §91.115 says that when operating on the water, the pilot must "insofar as possible, keep clear of all vessels and avoid impeding their navigation."

21. You (the seaplane) should give way, because you are deemed more maneuverable.

22. In this case, the right-of-way might be debatable; however, I would say that you should give way, because you are deemed more maneuverable.

23. The boats have the right-of-way.

24. The other vessel has the right-of-way in each of these three situations, because the seaplane is deemed more maneuverable.

25. A seaplane sailing power off is less maneuverable and should have the right-of-way—at least over any powered vessel.

26. a. Upstream = "returning." "Red right returning." The green buoy is on your left, as it should be. Yes, you are in the channel.

    b. Yes, when operating on the water, you are subject to the same navigational rules as any other watercraft.

128 An Aviator's Field Guide to the **Seaplane Rating**

27. In the Intracoastal Waterway (ICW) on the US East Coast, southbound = "returning" (by convention). "Red right returning." The red marker is on your right, as it should be. Yes, you are in the channel.

28. The aircraft taking off has the right-of-way over the one landing. You should go around.

29. **PAVE**:

    The **P**ilot (IMSAFE)

    The **A**ircraft (legal? airworthy?)

    The en**V**ironment (weather, water surface, obstructions, etc.)

    External circumstances/pressures (get-home-itis, pressure from pax)

30. For *any flight*, 14 CFR §91.103(b) requires pilots to know the runway (or waterway) lengths at their intended destination, and takeoff and landing distances under current conditions.

31. The preflight inspection for a seaplane and land plane are the same, except that in a seaplane you must additionally pump out and inspect the floats for structural integrity, and inspect the spreaders, the struts, the flying wires, and the water rudders and their associated cables and pulleys. If docked, inspecting the float on the side away from the dock may require turning the aircraft around.

32. The hose that runs from the pump-out port in the deck of the float to the bottom of the float compartment may have become disconnected from the port, so the pump has nothing to pump. If this occurs, the compartment could be full of water without you knowing. You must assume that that compartment contains too much water, and you must take the time to open the access hatch for that compartment to inspect the hose connection visually before taking off.

33. Even if the float is not damaged, there may be water in the float compartments from yesterday's flight, from rainwater seeping in from the deck overnight, or from water seeping through

Chapter 6—Oral Exam Preparation Questions   129

hull seams overnight. If there is water (which weighs 8 pounds per gallon) in the float compartments, it means you are almost certainly carrying considerable extra weight; at the very least, this will degrade performance and stability and could put you over maximum gross weight. If a compartment has been breached and is full of water, you will be unaware of this if you don't take the time to pump out the float compartments. And if you are flying an amphib, you won't see the pink, oily fluid that would let you know there is a hydraulic fluid leak.

34. Passenger briefing: "**SAFE**"

- **S**eatbelt operation; **S**econd pair of eyes: for traffic, and for landing gear position indicators
- **A**ir controls: cabin heat, cabin air; **A**irsickness bags
- **F**ire extinguisher location and operation
- **E**gress (how to operate doors and windows by feel, with eyes closed); **E**mergency equipment (including life jackets and survival kit); **E**mergency procedures

Self-briefing:

- Exit plan from dock or beach (if someone is available to help, *use them*)
- Planned path for takeoff run
- Abort point
- Altitude needed before turning back to the lake if engine fails

35. a. To enter Class C airspace, your aircraft must be equipped with a transponder and ADS-B Out.

  b. To do an LPV approach, your aircraft must be equipped with WAAS GPS.

36. *Answers will vary. Refer to your training aircraft's AFM/POH. An example answer is provided below for idle taxiing and step taxiing in the Seabird 1850/1850A.*

130 An Aviator's Field Guide to the **Seaplane Rating**

	Seabird 1850/1850A	
	Idle taxi	**Step taxi**
Throttle	1000 RPM	20"
Prop (if applicable)	Full forward	2500 RPM
Flaps	20°	20°
Stick position*	Full aft	Neutral
Pitch	N/A	5° up approx.
Water rudders (up/down)	Down	Up
Weathervaning tendency (normal/reverse)	Normal	Normal

*Exception: when idle taxiing downwind, the stick must be full forward.

37. The appearance of the water surface indicates that the wind is from the north at speeds in the low teens.

   a. Turning south to north while idle taxiing will be safe and quick, with a very small radius, because weathervaning will assist the turn.

   b. Turning north to south while idle taxiing may be impossible because weathervaning is counteracting your attempt to turn downwind. Your instinct will be to increase RPM, but that will only bury the bows of the floats. You could consider a plow taxi turn, but sailing backward is the better option.

38. From the water surface conditions, you can determine that the wind is from the north at approximately 10–12 knots.

   a. Yes, a step taxi turn from north to south can be done safely, though cautiously, in this situation. The forces in the turn will tend to tip the aircraft toward the outside of the turn (in this case, to windward), which is why you will hold full aileron in the direction of the turn. Meanwhile, the north wind will tend to tip the aircraft to leeward. These forces at least partially cancel each other out. I would make this turn with a large radius, and if at any point it felt unstable, I would immediately come off the step.

(continued)

Chapter 6—Oral Exam Preparation Questions **131**

b. A step taxi turn from south to north under these conditions is unsafe and should not be attempted: Both the wind and the forces of the turn will tend to capsize the aircraft to leeward. Come off the step and make an idle taxi turn to the north.

39. a. If you begin porpoising while step taxiing, you should immediately increase your pitch (up) by a few degrees, and if in a turn, increase your power by a couple of inches of MP.

b. If the porpoising does not stop after two oscillations, immediately pull power to idle, pull stick full aft, and come off the step.

40. You might consider making a plow taxi turn if you are taxiing to windward in a strong breeze and need to go downwind.

41. A plow taxi turn should be avoided because it is unstable (reverse weathervaning, risk of capsize), visibility is poor (steep deck angle), engine cooling is poor (high power/low speed), and the prop gets damaged by spray.

42. a. It is a small lake with a light breeze. You may not have enough room for a normal takeoff run. Consider step taxiing downwind and making a J-shaped turn to windward (only safe when the breeze is so light) so that by the time you're finished with the turn, you will be at, or near, flying speed and headed to windward with most of the lake still available.

b. This is too windy for a J-shaped step taxi turn. Sail downwind almost to the lee shore, and then do a rough water takeoff. When it is that windy, you should have plenty of room.

43. Point the ailerons in the direction you want to go, use opposite air rudder, and place water rudders up. So in this case, you would use full right aileron, full left air rudder, and water rudders up. You will sail southeastward, with the aircraft's longitudinal axis northwest–southeast.

44. a. **GUMPFARTS** before-takeoff checklist flow:

G = **G**as: fuel selector on both, quantity sufficient, boost
   pump to prime.

U = **U**ndercarriage: Landing gear up by all indicators.

M = **M**ixture: Best power.

P = **P**rop: Set for desired RPM (full forward for takeoff
   and landing).

F = **F**laps: 20° for normal takeoff.

A = **A**rea clear: Of obstructions, boaters, etc.

R = **R**udders (water): Down, then Up for takeoff.

T = **T**rim: Set for takeoff.

S = **S**tick: Full aft for takeoff.

b. *Answers will vary.*

45. *Answers will vary. Refer to your training aircraft's AFM/POH.
An example answer is provided below for the Seabird 1850A:*

	Seabird 1850A				
	A	**B**	**C**	**D**	**E**
Altitude (AGL)	500	500	500	Begin 500 ft/ min descent	Feet to inches
Throttle/prop (RPM)	20"/2500	15"/2500	15"/2500	Throttle as needed for 75 kt/ 500 fpm	Low power to touchdown, or idle
Flaps	0	20°	20°	20°	20°
Gear (amphib)	*UP*	*UP*	*UP*	*UP*	*UP*
Airspeed (KIAS)	100	75	75	75	75
Checklist/flow	GUMP-FARTS			"Mixture rich, prop full forward, gear is UP for water landing"	

Chapter 6—Oral Exam Preparation Questions **133**

46. a. Full right rudder with the water rudders down during initial application of full power. Then water rudders up and hand back to throttle.

   b. With air rudder, because you now have sufficient airspeed.

   c. If your pitch attitude is correct (in the 5°–8° pitch up range in the Seabird), and you have flying airspeed (about 55 knots in the Seabird), the aircraft will begin to feel light and will fly off without rotation.

   d. Try increasing your pitch a couple of degrees. You can lift one float (left float preferred), and you can "pop" the flaps briefly to 40° to help you break free. Be mindful of your abort point.

   e. Your training aircraft's V_Y = _____ (Refer to your training aircraft's AFM/POH.)

47. On the water, you will have normal weathervaning. Meanwhile, regardless of the direction of takeoff, you will have left-turning tendencies (P-factor, etc.). The weathervaning from a left crosswind will add to the aircraft's left-turning tendency from P-factor, etc., and the combined left-turning tendency may exceed the rudder's ability to maintain directional control. The weathervaning from a right crosswind, on the other hand, will counteract the left-turning tendency from P-factor, etc. Therefore, take off with a right crosswind.

48. See the factors discussed in the previous answer. An amphib seaplane on land, however, will have a reverse weathervaning tendency because the pivot point—the main gear—is relatively aft. A left crosswind will weathervane the aircraft to the right and will counteract the left-turning tendency due to P-factor, etc. Therefore, take off with a left crosswind.

49. You will have a right crosswind. You have no centerline to follow on the water, and if you go by the appearance of the water surface, you will touch down drifting to the left, which could well result in an accident. Instead, use the piling and the tree beyond as a "range"—if you keep them lined up with one another, you'll track in a straight line.

134 An Aviator's Field Guide to the **Seaplane Rating**

50. a. It will be a confined area takeoff. *(Refer to the AFM/POH and describe a confined area takeoff for your training aircraft.)*

b. Try increasing your pitch a little, lift one float, and pop the flaps—but be mindful of your abort point. If necessary, consider a wide J-shaped step taxi turn.

c. After liftoff, and having accelerated to V_X in ground effect, accelerate in the climb to at least "minimum maneuvering speed" (75 knots in the Seabird; _____ in your training aircraft) before turning, then continue a climbing spiral within the confines of the terrain until you have climbed clear of terrain.

51. This will be a confined area landing. *(Refer to the AFM/POH and describe a confined area landing for your training aircraft.)*

52. This will be a glassy water landing. It will be very difficult to judge your height above the water, and there is a risk of flying into the water or stalling above the water. You must use glassy water landing technique. *(Refer to the AFM/POH and describe the glassy water landing technique for your training aircraft.)*

53. a. The stillness of the water will make it harder to get airborne; surface tension makes it harder for the floats to break free of the water surface.

b. Before the takeoff run: Step taxi in circles (or have your friend do it in a boat) to create waves.

During the takeoff run: Lift one float (left preferred); consider popping the flaps.

c. As soon as you are free of the water surface, "go on instruments"—use the attitude indicator to ensure that you are maintaining a climb attitude, use the vertical speed indicator to ensure you are climbing, and use the airspeed indicator to ensure a stable climb airspeed.

54. This will be a rough water takeoff. *(Refer to the AFM/POH and describe a rough water takeoff for your training aircraft.)*

55. This will be a rough water landing. *(Refer to the AFM/POH and describe the rough water landing for your training aircraft.)*

56. A forward slip to a landing allows you to lose altitude without gaining airspeed. Hold ailerons one way (to windward if there is a crosswind) and use opposite rudder. Rudder is often the limiting factor: You may need full rudder and less than full aileron. The aircraft will track forward, but its longitudinal axis will not be aligned with the centerline. Nearing touchdown, or when you have lost the desired amount of altitude, ease out the aileron and rudder inputs.

57. This is intended to be a setup for a power-off 180° accuracy landing (Commercial: CA.IV.M), but in my view, in a floatplane (at least in the Seabird) there's scant difference between that and an emergency approach and landing (CA.IX.B). This is because without power, the Seabird descends so fast that it's not really about hitting an intended touchdown point; instead, it's about turning *immediately* toward the water and establishing and maintaining your best clean glide speed (85 KIAS in the Seabird) as you turn to windward for landing. This will require a significant pitch-down attitude, and as soon as you pitch up to prepare to touch down, your speed will bleed off very rapidly. You will have your hands full to avoid touching down much too hard from not reducing the pitch-down attitude quickly enough, and to avoid running out of airspeed and stalling above the water. Without power in a floatplane (at least in the Seabird), just making it to the water and achieving a reasonably smooth touchdown is the goal; an intended touchdown point is entirely secondary.

58. You need to make an emergency descent, and my goal with this question was to eliminate the landing itself and just focus on how to get from 6,000 feet to 1,000 feet (airport pattern altitude) as quickly as possible. You need to pull power off and hang out all the drag you can. Set throttle to idle, extend gear (amphib), extend flaps, pitch down to maintain airspeed at or below V_{FE}, bank 30–45°, and spiral downward to pattern altitude.

59. If you leave the dock with the wind from the east, the wind is going to weathervane you to the right—i.e., your tail will go left; if there are pilings or structures on the dock, your tail could strike them, causing damage. If someone is available to help, use them to keep your tail from being blown toward the dock until you are completely free of the dock. You could also have them hold the tail and position you directly to windward (perpendicular to the dock) before you start the engine.

If you leave the dock with the wind from the west—Now the wind is going to weathervane your nose (and propeller) toward the dock and the tail away from the dock. I would suggest getting help to have someone hold the tail to position the aircraft perpendicular to the dock, pointing eastward, before starting the engine.

60. You want to dock with a headwind (or headwind component), because it will help you come to a stop. There are several docking options in this scenario, but the one you chose may be the simplest, for two reasons. First, docking with your left float alongside the dock means you will not have to move over to the right seat as you approach the dock. Second, as you approach the dock at an angle (heading roughly north–northwest), the wind will help weathervane you parallel to the dock.

So, with all the preliminaries taken care of (avionics power off, master off, headset off and stowed [including cord], seatbelt off, door open, left foot out on the step, right foot on rudders, power at idle, right hand on mixture), approach the dock at maybe a 30-degree angle. When about two float lengths from the dock (or less if the breeze is strong), turn northward enough so that the bow of the left float will not strike the dock. If the wind were from the north, you would turn parallel to the dock; but in this case you don't need to, and shouldn't, turn parallel to the dock, because the northeast wind will bring your tail to the dock. Then you can just hop out and secure those dock lines.

61. It is better to sail backward than to do a plow taxi turn followed by a step taxi downwind in rough water. But when sailing, you don't go directly downwind: you go downwind at an angle (something like 45°) one direction or another. Therefore, you need to zigzag downwind, in a manner similar to a sailor tacking. Sail in one direction (water rudders up, ailerons in the direction you want the plane to move, rudder in the opposite direction), then reverse the controls and sail in the other direction, sailing back and forth until you get to your beach.

Chapter 7
Preparing for the Practical Test

The examiner is required to follow the *Private Pilot for Airplane Category Airman Certification Standards* (FAA-S-ACS-6) or the *Commercial Pilot for Airplane Category Airman Certification Standards* (FAA-S-ACS-7), depending on what certificate you currently hold. Each task defined in the ACS includes knowledge, risk management, and skill elements. In Appendix 1 of both the Private and Commercial ACS is a grid that shows what specific tasks ASES candidates are responsible for when adding an ASES rating to an existing pilot certificate. (Pilots who currently hold a multi-engine rating are responsible for a few ACS tasks that single-engine-rated pilots are not responsible for, even though the seaplane rating you are training for is a *single*-engine seaplane rating.) These grids are summarized for your instructor in this book's preface and Appendix A.

While your practical test will generally be a test of your knowledge and your ability to operate a seaplane safely and properly, you can count on being tested on the tasks indicated in the grid. On the flight test, pilots holding a Private Pilot Certificate will be held to Private ACS standards, and those holding a Commercial Pilot Certificate will be held to Commercial ACS standards.

The ground and flight lessons in the ASES Syllabus (Chapter 2) and the Oral Exam Preparation Questions (Chapter 6) in this book are designed to address all of the tasks you will be responsible for on your practical test. Please review the ASES add-on grid in the

Private or Commercial ACS (depending on what certificate you hold) to verify your required tasks. If your instructor's ground and flight training has addressed all of your ACS-required tasks, and if you have read the Study Guide (Chapter 5) and can answer the oral exam preparation questions in this book, you can approach the practical test with confidence that you are well prepared.

You will need to bring your logbook, pilot certificate, current medical certificate, photo ID, the aircraft logbooks, payment for the examiner's fee, and anything else your instructor recommends. Wear shoes and clothes that you can get wet.

Before the practical test, you will need to submit your IACRA application online, and then your instructor will need to recommend you for the practical test in IACRA. It is best to do all of this the day before the practical test so that neither you nor your instructor will have the stress of scrambling to fix IACRA issues the day of the practical test.

You will need certain endorsements in your logbook before the practical test. These are outlined for your instructor in this book's preface.

Make sure you understand clearly from your instructor what you will be expected to bring with you to the practical test.

The practical test will consist of an oral examination and a flight test. If things are going well, these often take about an hour each, but the examiner will take whatever time they feel is needed.

We all want to know in advance what we're going to be tested on, and in the case of an FAA practical test for an ASES add-on rating, the real answer is that you should be prepared to discuss/perform the knowledge, risk management, and skill elements of all of your required tasks from the ASES add-on grid in the Private or Commercial ACS (depending on the certificate you currently hold).

The tasks required of *all* ASES add-on candidates are listed beginning on page xv of this book. Please review that list, at a minimum. That list is followed by two tasks that are required of all private (but only some commercial) ASES add-on candidates. And in Appendix A you will find, in addition to the grids themselves, listings of required tasks for other subgroups of ASES add-on candidates.

140 An Aviator's Field Guide to the **Seaplane Rating**

If your instructor has sent ASES candidates to this examiner before, they may be able to pass along feedback regarding the checkrides from those candidates, and that can be very helpful—but just remember that even if previous candidates weren't tested on a certain task, that does not mean you won't be. If it is a required task, be prepared for it.

Unless your instructor tells you specifically that you won't be asked for it, you might consider doing a weight and balance in advance for your training aircraft, with you and the examiner and a realistic amount of fuel on board. It's much easier to complete weight and balance calculations in the hotel room than in front of the examiner.

Note that the examiner may check off some skills elements during the oral examination. For example, you could be asked to discuss how you'd handle various emergencies, instead of having to deal with them in flight. And if you're in that subgroup for whom commercial maneuvers are a required task, if you're lucky the examiner may ask you to describe how to do Lazy Eights instead of making you do them in the airplane.

As with any FAA oral examination, if you don't know the answer, don't make something up. If you don't know the answer but you know where to find it, then look it up.

As with any FAA flight test, there is no expectation that every maneuver will be performed perfectly, though they must be within limits. If during the performance of a maneuver you recognize that you are not within limits, acknowledge it to the examiner and tell them that you would like to start that maneuver over. The examiner will usually let you do so, and the ACS itself suggests that they should: In Appendix 1 of both the Private and Commercial ACS, in the section describing what constitutes "unsatisfactory performance," the criteria include "*Consistently* exceeding tolerances stated in the skills elements of the Task" (italics mine) and "Failure to take prompt corrective action *when* tolerances are exceeded" (italics mine). Thus, the ACS itself acknowledges that you may not do everything within limits the first time. If you are consistently not within limits, and if you fail to take prompt corrective action, the

Chapter 7—Preparing for the Practical Test **141**

examiner will not be able to pass you. But *do not* throw in the towel if a maneuver or two is not within limits on your first attempt.

And always—checkride or not—if you are unstable on final approach, *go around*.

Chapter 8
Congratulations— You Earned Your Seaplane Rating! Now What?

You may have gotten your seaplane rating for the sheer fun of it, or as part of a goal to get all the ratings you can, with no intent ever to fly floats again. There's nothing wrong with that at all, and if that's the case, I hope you had a blast learning to fly floats.

But if you do want to do more float flying, what are your options, assuming that you are not going to buy your own seaplane?

First, a very limited number of places in the United States will let you rent seaplanes. Many operators' insurance companies will require you to have a certain number of hours in type in order to rent their aircraft, though some may only require you to have a certain number of hours in seaplanes.

As published in the 2024 Seaplane Pilots Association *Seaplane Training Guide*, the list in Table 8-1 shows where you can currently rent a seaplane in the United States without an instructor.[1]

---

[1] "Flight Training Guide," Seaplane Pilots Association, accessed December 4, 2024, https://seaplanepilotsassociation.org/flight-schools/.

Table 8-1. Seaplane Rentals Available in the United States

State	Organization	Aircraft
California	San Diego Seaplanes	Republic Seabee amphib
	Los Angeles/Long Beach Seaplanes (same owner)	Cessna 182 amphib Helio Courier amphib
	High Flight Aviation	Lake amphib
Florida	Flying Fish, LLC	SeaRey amphib
	Sunair Aviation	Aviat Husky amphib
Indiana	Mac's Seaplane Service	Cessna 140
Michigan	Northwestern Michigan College	Piper Super Cub amphib
Minnesota	Air Trek North	Cessna 172 amphib
Missouri	Flying Fish, LLC	SeaRey amphib
New York	Rochester Air Center	Cessna 172 amphib
Washington	Bluegreen Xtreme, Oceanfloats	Custom T-I-I amphib
	Seaplane Scenics and Adventures in Flight	Cessna 172 straight

International options for solo seaplane rental include two operators in British Columbia, Canada; two in Ontario, Canada; and one at Lake Como, Italy.

Of course, check with your instructor in case solo rental is an unpublished option offered for students at the location where you trained.

Other than those limited solo rental options, to maintain the seaplane skills you've learned, you will need to visit your local seaplane instructor for more dual instruction from time to time. And in addition to maintaining what you've already learned, you can add to those skills. Consider these options:

- Take a couple of hours of seaplane training each year as a refresher.

- Take your flight review in a seaplane. (Note that the AOPA Air Safety Institute has a Focused Flight Review designed for

144 An Aviator's Field Guide to the **Seaplane Rating**

seaplanes.[2]) Can you get your flight review done less expensively in a landplane? Absolutely. But will it be as much fun? Not a chance!

- Take advanced seaplane instruction if your current instructor offers it. Or consider taking a course such the Seaplane Safety Institute at Southern Seaplane in Louisiana.[3]

- Take transition training in an amphib if you earned your rating on straight floats.

- Accomplish a WINGS task in a seaplane (FAA Safety Team's WINGS Pilot Proficiency Program[4]). The WINGS program for seaplanes is called SeaWINGS, and you get a special SeaWINGS pin for achieving a level of WINGS in a seaplane.

- Pursue your Multi-Engine Sea Rating. If you thought your ASEL training was expensive, this will be even more so! However, Lockwood Aviation in Florida and WaterWings in Alabama have now been licensed by the FAA to offer AMES training in an Aircam twin seaplane, at a fraction of the cost of other multi-engine seaplanes.[5] Note that pilots must already hold an AMEL certificate to use the Aircam AMES option.

For further learning, consider the following reading and video resources:

- *How to Fly Floats*, by the late J. J. Frey. Mr. Frey had expertise in all aspects of flying and maintaining floatplanes and was eager

---

[2] "Focused Flight Review," Aircraft Owners and Pilots Association (AOPA), accessed August 22, 2024, https://www.aopa.org/training-and-safety/active-pilots/focused-flight-review.

[3] "Seaplane Safety Institute," Southern Seaplane, Inc., accessed August 22, 2024, https://www.southernseaplane.com/seaplane-safety-institute.html.

[4] "WINGS—Pilot Proficiency Program," Federal Aviation Administration, FAA Safety Team (FAASTeam), accessed August 22, 2024, https://www.faasafety.gov/wings/pub/learn_more.aspx.

[5] "Multi-Engine Seaplane Training," Sebring Aviation, accessed December 4, 2024, https://www.sebring-aviation.com/pilot-training/multi-engine-seaplane-ames; "Multi Engine Seaplane Ratings," WaterWings Seaplanes, accessed December 4, 2024, https://www.waterwings.com/multi-engine-sea-ratings.

Chapter 8—You Earned Your Seaplane Rating! Now What? **145**

to help floatplane pilots with their questions and problems. His little book contains a wealth of knowledge.

- *Notes of a Seaplane Instructor: An Instructional Guide to Seaplane Flying*, by Burke Mees. This book is a distillation of the author's decades of experience as a seaplane instructor, and it takes you far beyond what most people learn when training for ASES. It helped me better understand *why* we do things the way we do them in seaplanes, and it also explained the importance of some factors I hadn't even considered. It will help make you a better and safer seaplane pilot.

- "Avoiding Ultimate Static Stability," by Dave Hensch of Florida Seaplanes, in the September/October 2019 issue of *Water Flying* magazine (the magazine of the Seaplane Pilots Association). Among other things, this excellent article explains why pilots must avoid landing *flat and fast* in seaplanes. Part II appeared in the November/December 2019 issue of *Water Flying*.[6]

- FAA Advisory Circular (AC) 91-69, *Seaplane Safety for 14 CFR Part 91 Operators*. This AC includes sections on preflight inspection, passenger briefing (with a sample in the appendix), seatbelt/shoulder harness usage, escape/egress, water survival, and flotation gear.

- The *Seaplane Ops Guide* booklet produced by the Alaskan Region FAASTeam and available at www.faasafety.gov. You won't find anything here that you don't already know, but it's a nice and concise summary/review.

- The Seaplane Pilots Association (SPA) Online Training webpage offers resources to encourage and enhance safe operations within the seaplane community. Its "Amphibious Aircraft Gear Management Best Practices" document and "Safe Amphibious Gear Operations" video help pilots understand the

---

[6] Dave Hensch, "Avoiding Ultimate Static Stability: How to not go upside down in a seaplane," pt. 1, *Water Flying*, September/October 2019, 16–23, https://digitaleditions.walsworth.com/publication/?i=618024&p=18; pt. 2, *Water Flying*, November/December 2019, 18–25, https://digitaleditions.walsworth.com/publication/?i=638448&p=20.

factors that can lead to a gear-down water landing and provide guidance and methods to avoid those factors. Both are available at seaplanepilotsassociation.org/online-training/.

And while you're considering the above options, I strongly recommend that you join the Seaplane Pilots Association (SPA) (seaplanepilotsassociation.org). There are many membership benefits, including the monthly *Water Flying* magazine, which will keep you thinking (and dreaming) like a seaplane pilot; the annual *Seaplane Training Guide*, which was the source of the above list showing all of the places you can train (and in some cases rent), including aircraft types and costs; and the Water Landing Directory app, which lets you know which waterways are open to seaplanes and which ones are not, where you can get fuel on the water, etc. And the SPA advocates continually on behalf of seaplane pilots—for example, to keep waterways we can currently use open to seaplanes and to open up waterways that are currently closed to seaplanes.

I hope the skills you learned during your seaplane training will make you a better and safer pilot, no matter what kind of flying you do. Fly safe!

Appendix A
More Than You
May Want to Know
About the ACS

In the Seaplane Instructor's Guide to the ACS on page xiv of this book, I list the required ACS tasks for ASES add-on candidates who currently hold an ASES rating, with or without AMEL. Here I present more detail regarding how I arrived at those conclusions, and how to use the ACS to determine required tasks for other pilots.

Appendix 1 of each ACS contains several grids. In the *Private Pilot for Airplane Category Airman Certification Standards* (FAA-S-ACS-6C), the relevant grid in Appendix 1 is titled "Addition of an Airplane Single-Engine Sea Rating to an Existing Private Pilot Certificate." In the *Commercial Pilot for Airplane Category Airman Certification Standards* (FAA-S-ACS-7B), the relevant grid in Appendix 1 is titled "Addition of an Airplane Single-Engine Sea Rating to an existing Commercial Pilot Certificate."

As explained in the Seaplane Instructor's Guide to the ACS, there is no such thing as an ATP ASES add-on, so if your ASES add-on student currently holds a land ATP Certificate, they will be getting a *commercial* ASES add-on (not an ATP ASES certificate) and will be held to Commercial ACS standards on the checkride.

Comparing the Private ACS and Commercial ACS overall (unrelated to seaplane training) reveals that they are mostly, though not entirely, parallel. For example, in Area of Operation IV (Takeoffs,

149

Landings, and Go-Arounds), Task A is "Normal Takeoff and Climb" in both the Private and Commercial ACS. Although in some cases there are differences in completion standards for private and commercial pilots, in Areas of Operation I–VII, the Private and Commercial ACSs follow the same parallel outline, with a few exceptions. For example, Area of Operation IV, Task M, is "Forward Slip to a Landing" in the Private ACS but "Power-Off 180° Accuracy Approach and Landing" in the Commercial ACS. Area of Operation V is "Performance Maneuvers" in both the Private and Commercial ACS, but there are more tasks, and different tasks, in the Commercial ACS than in the Private ACS for that area of operation. In the Private ACS, Area of Operation VIII is "Basic Instrument Maneuvers," whereas in the Commercial ACS it is "High-Altitude Operations." Areas of Operation IX (Emergency Operations) and X (Multiengine Operations) are the same in the Private and Commercial ACS. The Private ACS finishes with Areas of Operation XI (Night Operations) and XII (Postflight Procedures), whereas the Commercial ACS skips night operations and finishes with Area of Operation XI (Postflight Procedures).

Now let's get back to how all of this applies to seaplane training. The grids referred to above show that the areas of operation your student will be responsible for depend not only on whether the student holds a Private or Commercial Pilot Certificate but also on whether the student has a Multi-Engine Rating: The requirements for those who hold AMEL (even though they are training for Airplane *Single*-Engine Sea, not Airplane *Multi*-Engine Sea) are slightly different in some areas of operation.

First let's combine and reorganize those grids to reflect all of the above, as shown in Table A-1.

A very important nuance must be noted in order to interpret these grids correctly. The AMEL columns in the private and commercial ASES add-on grids refer *only* to pilots who hold AMEL but *who **do not** also hold ASEL*. If a pilot holds both ASEL and AMEL ratings—which is the case for the vast majority of pilots who hold AMEL ratings—the required tasks are those in the ASEL column, *not* those in the AMEL column.

150   Appendix A

Table A-1. ACS Areas of Operation and Tasks Required for ASES Applicants Based on Current Certificate and Rating Held

Area of operation	Certificate and rating currently held			
	Private		Commercial	
	ASEL	AMEL*	ASEL	AMEL*
	Tasks required			
I	F, G, I	F, G, I	F, G, I	F, G, I
II	A, B, E, F	A, B, E, F	A, B, E, F	A, B, E, F
III	B	B	B	B
IV	A, B, G, H, I, J, K, L	A, B, G, H, I, J, K, L, M	A, B, G, H, I, J, K, L	A, B, G, H, I, J, K, L, M
V	None	None	None	B; C or D; E
VI	None	None	None	None
VII	None	None	None	None
VIII	None	None	None	None
IX	A, B	A, B	None	B, C
X	None	None	None	None
XI	None	None	B	B
XII	B	B	N/A	N/A

* These tasks are required only for ASES add-on candidates who hold an AMEL rating but do not hold an ASEL rating.

So, for example, look at Area of Operation IX in the grid for commercial ASES add-on candidates. In the ASEL column we find "None," but in the AMEL column we find "B, C." So if you hold a Commercial Pilot Certificate with ASEL, it is clear that you will have no required tasks in Area of Operation IX. And if you have AMEL, it appears from the grid that you are responsible for tasks B and C in Area of Operation IX, right? *Only if you hold AMEL **without** ASEL.* If you hold ASEL as well as AMEL, your required tasks are the ones in the ASEL column—namely "None."

Another example: In Area of Operation IV for both private and commercial pilots, the ASEL required tasks are A, B, G, H, I, J, K, and L, whereas the AMEL required tasks are those same tasks plus Task M. So are private and commercial ASES add-on candidates who hold AMEL responsible for Task M? *Only if they do not also hold*

Appendix A   151

ASEL. So only those who hold AMEL *without* ASEL are responsible for Task M in Area of Operation IV.

And as noted above, in the Private ACS Area of Operation IV Task M is "Forward Slip to a Landing," whereas in the Commercial ACS Area of Operation IV Task M is "Power-Off 180° Accuracy Approach and Landing." So, in addition to tasks A, B, G, H, I, J, K, and L, private pilots who hold AMEL without ASEL are required to demonstrate forward slip to a landing, and commercial pilots who hold AMEL without ASEL are required to demonstrate power-off 180° accuracy approach and landing. But the vast majority of pilots who hold AMEL will not be required to demonstrate *either* task, because they also hold ASEL and thus will only be responsible for the tasks in the ASEL column, which do not include Task M.

Another example: In Area of Operation V in the commercial ASES add-on grid, we find "None" in the ASEL column and "B; C or D; E" in the AMEL column. So is your commercial ASES add-on candidate who holds AMEL really going to have to demonstrate lazy eights and other maneuvers in the seaplane on the checkride? *Only if they do not also hold ASEL*—because if they also hold ASEL, the pertinent column is the ASEL column, which has no required tasks in Area of Operation V.

In the Seaplane Instructor's Guide to the ACS, I summarized who is responsible for what tasks, excluding those rare pilots who hold AMEL *without* ASEL. Now let's summarize the requirements for that exclusive group (pilots who hold AMEL without ASEL):

- In addition to the tasks other private pilots will be responsible for, **private** ASES add-on candidates who hold AMEL without ASEL will be responsible for demonstrating:
  - Forward Slip to a Landing (Private ACS Area of Operation IV, Task M).

- In addition to the tasks other commercial pilots will be responsible for, **commercial** ASES add-on candidates who hold AMEL without ASEL will be responsible for:
  - Power-Off 180° Accuracy Approach and Landing (Commercial ACS Area of Operation IV, Task M)
  - Steep Spiral *and* either Chandelles or Lazy Eights *and* Eights on Pylons (Commercial ACS Area of Operation V, Tasks B; C or D; and E)
  - Emergency Approach and Landing (Simulated) (Commercial ACS Area of Operation IX, Task B)
  - Systems and Equipment Malfunctions (Commercial ACS Area of Operation IX, Task C)

Several differences in the requirements for private vs. commercial ASES add-on candidates, and the biggest changes in the latest revision of the ACS, are in Area of Operation IX (Emergency Operations). The grids show that Task A, Emergency Descent, is a required task only for private pilots (ASEL with or without AMEL). Task B, Emergency Approach and Landing (Simulated) is a required task for all candidates *except* ASEL-only commercial pilots. And Task C, Systems and Equipment Malfunctions, is a required task only for AMEL-rated commercial pilots *who do not also hold ASEL*.

And finally, whereas in the grids, Areas XI and XII for private vs. commercial pilots appear to address different tasks, recall that Private Area of Operation XII is the same as Commercial Area of Operation XI (both are Postflight Procedures), so all ASES add-on candidates (private, commercial, ASEL and/or AMEL) are responsible for Task B (Seaplane Post-Landing Procedures).

Table A-2 on the next page summarizes the ACS tasks that are required of some but not all ASES add-on candidates.

Appendix A   153

Table A-2. ACS Tasks Required of Some but Not All ASES Add-On Candidates

ACS code	Task	All Private ASEL and/or AMEL	Private AMEL without ASEL	Commercial AMEL without ASEL
PA.IV.M	Forward slip to a landing		X	
CA.IV.M	Power-off 180° accuracy approach and landing			X
CA.V.B; CA.V.C or D; CA.V.E	Steep spiral; chandelles or lazy eights; eights on pylons			X
PA.IX.A CA.IX.A	Emergency descent	X		
PA.IX.B CA.IX.B	Emergency approach and landing (simulated)	X		X
CA.IX.C	Systems and equipment malfunctions			X

Appendix B
A Sampling of Seaplane Checklist Mnemonics

The following are some mnemonics used in various seaplane training programs, intended to help you remember what you need to do in each phase of a flight in a seaplane.

As you will see from this collection (which is only a small subset of the mnemonics that are in use), there is overlap: One school's GUMP is another's GUMP-C, for example. And **G** may represent **G**as in one mnemonic and **G**ear in another. And some of the associations in these mnemonics may seem like a stretch: I for one will not be thinking "runup" when I see **A** in a mnemonic if it stands for "**A**irplane runup," as it does in one of the mnemonics below. You may find that in some cases it could be harder to remember the mnemonic than to remember the items the mnemonic is supposed to help you remember!

You will also notice that some mnemonics contain items that do not pertain to your training aircraft. If you are training in a straight-float J-3 Cub, you don't need to remember items related to landing gear and propeller control, for example. If the engine of your training aircraft is fuel-injected, you don't need carburetor heat in your mnemonic. Conversely, a mnemonic that is appropriate for the straight-float Cub will be inadequate for a complex amphib.

In this book, I use GUMPFARTS both before takeoff and before landing. I first saw this mnemonic in a *Water Flying* article by Dave Hensch of Florida Seaplanes, Inc. (When I took my ASES training

155

with Dave's father, Rich Hensch, the all-purpose mnemonic used at Florida Seaplanes was just FARTS.) GUMPFARTS is appropriate to the Seabird (the fictitious aircraft used as an example in this book), which has a fuel-injected engine with a controllable-pitch propeller, and (in the case of the Seabird amphib) amphibious floats. And in the study guide and checklists in this book, I do not present separate mnemonics for before-landing inspection of the water surface, docking, etc.; you will find examples of such mnemonics below.

For each mnemonic, I list a school or association that either developed the mnemonic or uses it. Most of these mnemonics are likely used, as presented here or with variations, in many schools in addition to the ones I have listed. I am not aware of any mnemonics that are proprietary.

But your ASES instructor has already chosen mnemonics that are appropriate to your training aircraft, and which fit with what and how they teach. During your training, and until you gain substantial seaplane flying experience on your own after you get your ASES rating, *use the mnemonic(s) your instructor recommends.* With time and experience, you may find that mnemonics other than or in addition to the ones you used during your training may be helpful— and you may even come up with your own mnemonics. For now, though, keep it simple and use what your instructor recommends.

And finally, keep in mind that all checklist mnemonics are simply ways to help you remember what's on your aircraft's FAA-approved checklist and help keep you out of trouble. So ultimately, with or without a mnemonic, you are responsible for doing everything that's on your aircraft's formal checklist, and for using good judgment.

Before Takeoff

GUMPFARTS

(Florida Seaplanes, Inc.)
    Gas: fuel selector on BOTH, fuel pump as required
    Undercarriage: gear UP for water takeoff
    Mixture: best power
    Prop: full forward

Flaps: set for takeoff
Area clear of traffic (boaters or aircraft) and obstructions, including power lines
(Water) Rudders: UP
Trim: SET for takeoff
Stick (control wheel): full aft

GLUMPS

(Aqua Aero, LLC)
Gas: proper tank
Landing lights: ON
Undercarriage (wheels and water rudders): UP
Mixture: rich
Propeller: forward
Seat belts: fastened

CIGAR (CIGGARRR)

(Seaplane Pilots Association, *Amphibious Aircraft Gear Management Best Practices*)
Controls: free and clear
Instruments: check each instrument for proper setting
Gas: fullest tank
Gear: remind yourself "Positive rate—Gear UP."
Attitude: check trim and flaps
Runup: perform runup
Radio: make radio call
Rudder: raise water rudder

CIGARS

(Sebring Aviation, Inc.)
Controls: free and correct
Instruments: check
Gas: check quantity and proper tank
Airplane: runup
Radios: set
Switches: Lights/fuel pump on, canopy closed (if so equipped)

Takeoff

GRAF
(WaterWings Seaplanes, LLC)
    Gear: UP for water takeoff, DOWN for runway takeoff
    Rudders (water): UP
    Area: clear
    Flaps: set for takeoff

FATS
(Sebring Aviation, Inc.)
    Flaps: set for takeoff
    Area: clear
    Trim: set for takeoff
    Stick: full aft

FARTY
(Aqua Aero, LLC)
    Flaps: set
    Area: clear
    Ailerons: into wind
    Rudders: set
    Trim: set
    Yoke: back

CARS
(Jack Brown's Seaplane Base)
    Controls: free and correct
    Area: clear
    Rudders (water): UP
    Stick: full aft

CAR
(Southern Maryland Seaplanes)
    Configuration: landing gear UP for water takeoff, then flow to
        check cockpit settings, aft to forward, right to left
    Area: inspect (wind, traffic, takeoff path)
    Rudders (water): UP

Cruise

GUMP

(Seaplane Pilots Association *Amphibious Aircraft Gear Management Best Practices*)

Gas: confirm fuel selector position
Undercarriage: check to make sure gear is UP
Mixture: lean if necessary
Propeller: check for proper setting

Before Landing (Surveying Landing Area)

WLNOT

(Sebring Aviation, Inc.)

Water depth and conditions
Lane length
Noise abatement
Obstructions (both on and under the surface)
Towers, terrain, and traffic

WOODS

(Aqua Aero, LLC)

Wind direction
Obstacles
Objects in water
Depth of water
Size of area

Landing

GUMPFARTS

(Florida Seaplanes, Inc.)

Gas: fuel selector on BOTH, fuel pump as required

Undercarriage: gear UP for water landing, DOWN for runway landing

Mixture: best power

Prop: full forward

Flaps: set for landing

Area clear of traffic (boaters or aircraft) and obstructions, including power lines

(Water) **R**udders: UP

Trim: SET for landing

Stick (control wheel): pitch for approach airspeed

GUMP-C

(Seaplane Pilots Association *Amphibious Aircraft Gear Management Best Practices*)

Three times: (1) on **downwind** (or first application of flaps if straight-in), (2) **base** (or when stabilized on approach if straight-in), and (3) **final approach** (or when flaps are moved to final landing setting if straight-in).

Gas: check for fullest tank

Undercarriage: *position* gear (up for water landing, down for runway landing) on downwind; *check* gear position on base and again on final

Mixture: full rich

Prop: set to high RPM

Carb heat: apply (if applicable)

GIFFTS

(Sebring Aviation, Inc.)

Gear: appropriate position (up for water landing, down for runway landing) by all indicators

Instruments: check engine instruments, altitude, airspeed

Fuel pumps: ON

Flaps: as desired

Trim: set

Speed: correct for type of landing

GRAF

(WaterWings Seaplanes, LLC)

Gear: appropriate position (UP for water landing, DOWN for runway landing) by all indicators

Rudders (water): UP

Area: clear

Flaps: set for landing

CAR

(Southern Maryland Seaplanes)

Configuration: landing gear UP for water landing, then flow to check cockpit settings, aft to forward, right to left

Area: inspect (wind, traffic, landing area including intended touchdown point)

Rudders (water): UP

Docking

4 H's

(Aqua Aero, LLC)

Hatch: door open

Headset: removed and stowed, especially the cables

Harness: off and stowed

Hats: secured or stowed

Appendix B   161

Shutdown

4 M's
(Aqua Aero, LLC)
    Music: Radios and avionics OFF
    Mixture: Cutoff
    Master: OFF
    Magnetos: OFF

* * *

Appendix B References

- **Aqua Aero, LLC:** aqua-aero.com
- **Florida Seaplanes, Inc.:** flyfloatplanes.com
- **Jack Brown's Seaplane Base:** brownsseaplane.com
- **Seaplane Pilots Association:** seaplanepilotsassociation.org
- **Sebring Aviation:** sebring-aviation.com
- **Southern Maryland Seaplanes:** somdseaplanes.com
- **Southern Seaplane, Inc.:** southernseaplane.com
- **WaterWings Seaplanes, LLC:** waterwings.com

Appendix C:
More on Winds and Currents

In the Study Guide sections on water takeoffs and water landings, I gave general guidance regarding the best and worst combinations of wind and current for both takeoff and landing, and I said that further discussion was beyond the scope of this course.

Here is that further discussion. You don't need it for your initial ASES training, especially if (as is usually the case) you train on small- to moderate-size lakes where current is negligible. But as a rated seaplane pilot, you may find yourself operating in rivers or in tidal areas where current is a factor, and it is worth thinking about how the presence of current may affect your decision-making regarding water takeoffs and landings. It turns out that it *does* matter whether you take off or land with or against the current, and the "right" answer may surprise you. Current will also affect your decisions regarding taxiing after touchdown and your options for docking.

But before looking at the effects of current, let's review some basics.

As land plane pilots, we learned very early about airspeed (the speed of the aircraft relative to the air) and groundspeed (the speed of the aircraft relative to the ground). We were taught to take off and land into the wind whenever possible. Let's review why. We know that the aircraft needs a certain airspeed to take off—regardless of wind speed or direction. And the aircraft will stop flying (ideally

163

when we land!) when airspeed falls below a certain level, again regardless of wind speed and direction.

But the amount of runway we consume for takeoff and landing is very much affected by wind speed and by the direction of the wind relative to the aircraft. For takeoff in a land plane, we will achieve flying airspeed sooner when headed into the wind, so our takeoff run will be shorter—i.e., we will use less runway. And regarding landings: Our groundspeed for approach and landing will be lower if headed into the wind, so we will land in a shorter distance over the ground and with less chance of damage when we contact the ground.

Waterspeed

All of the above is as true for seaplane operations as for land plane operations, and for the same reasons. But there is an additional factor to consider when making a takeoff from or landing on the water, and it has to do with the drag exerted on the floats by the water. This is determined by the speed at which the floats are moving relative to the water surface while in contact with the water, which (not having seen a name for it elsewhere) I will call *waterspeed*.

How do you determine your waterspeed? That depends on whether there is *current*, which just means movement of water over the earth's surface, as in a river or a tidal zone. If there is no current (as is the case on a lake, for example), waterspeed and groundspeed are the same. But if there is current, waterspeed is *the net effect of your groundspeed* (how fast you're moving relative to the earth's surface) *and the current* (how fast the water is moving relative to the earth's surface).

If we assume for simplicity that we are in a narrow river, so our only options are to take off or land with the current or against the current, then the current will be either added to or subtracted from our groundspeed to calculate our waterspeed. If we are moving against the current (i.e., upstream), our waterspeed is our groundspeed *plus* the speed of the current; if we are moving with the current (i.e., downstream) our waterspeed is our groundspeed *minus* the speed of the current.

So let's say our aircraft stalls at an airspeed of 60 knots, we're going to land in a river with a current of 5 knots, and there's no wind (so our groundspeed equals our airspeed). If we land against the current (i.e., upstream), our waterspeed at touchdown is 60 knots + 5 knots = 65 knots. And if we land with the current (i.e., downstream), our waterspeed is 60 knots – 5 knots = 55 knots —i.e., 10 knots less than if we had landed upstream.

To summarize:

Groundspeed = **airspeed *minus* headwind, or *plus* tailwind.**
Waterspeed = **groundspeed *plus* current upstream, or *minus* current downstream.**

Notice that taking off or landing into a headwind *reduces* your groundspeed, which is good, but taking off or landing a seaplane into a current (i.e., upstream) *increases* your waterspeed, which is bad (see below).

Vector diagrams may help you see *why* waterspeed is groundspeed ± current (and how to choose whether to add or subtract current without having to remember a formula), but I will spare you the vectors for now.

Why Waterspeed Matters

We will look at numerical examples shortly, but first, let's think about why we need to know waterspeed.

Just as in a land plane, a seaplane's *airspeed* dictates performance: factors such as when the aircraft stalls, when it will become airborne, and how fast we can safely fly in turbulence; and in a seaplane just as in a land plane, *groundspeed* dictates things such as how much runway we will need to take off or land, and how bad the damage will be if we collide with something on the ground.

But what does waterspeed dictate? It dictates the amount of frictional drag the water exerts on the floats. The greater the waterspeed, the greater the drag. On a runway, there is not appreciably more rolling resistance from the tires on the runway at high speed than at low speed. This is not the case on the water: The faster the floats are moving relative to the water surface—i.e.,

Appendix C   165

the greater the waterspeed—the greater is the drag on the floats from the water.

And why does that matter? First, the more frictional drag acting on the floats, the longer it will take for the seaplane to get off the water, because the drag on the floats slows the plane's acceleration to liftoff airspeed. With enough thrust, we will get there eventually—but it will take longer, and we may run out of lake. Second, frictional drag on the floats causes a nose-down pitching moment, which moves the center of buoyancy (CB) on the floats—the point about which a seaplane on the water yaws—forward. If the center of buoyancy moves forward, our directional stability decreases (as explained in Chapter 8 of *Notes of a Seaplane Instructor* by Burke Mees): Our seaplane becomes like a taildragger, with the center of gravity aft of the pivot point—and whereas in a taildragger on the runway this can result in a ground loop, in a seaplane on the water it can result in a "waterloop" and possibly a capsize. This is especially important when landing: Ideally we'd like to touch down with the lowest waterspeed possible. (Now you may see why Dave Hensch warns against landing *flat* and *fast*—a warning I repeat in the Study Guide: When we land flat instead of on the steps of the floats, the CB is already forward of where it should be, which reduces our directional stability. And if we land fast, the frictional drag is also higher, moving the CB even farther forward, further increasing the risk of a waterloop due to loss of directional stability. And that nose-down pitching moment could bury the bows of the floats, causing the aircraft to pitchpole.) And on takeoff, we want the lowest waterspeed possible to minimize frictional drag on the floats, so we can achieve flying airspeed sooner.

How can we minimize waterspeed on takeoff and landing? If we have only wind to consider (such as on a lake), we will *take off and land into the wind* (unless the width of the lake is too small in the windward direction, in which case we will make a crosswind takeoff or landing—but never downwind). With zero current, waterspeed = groundspeed = airspeed minus headwind. So if our airspeed is 60 knots and we have a 10-knot headwind, our groundspeed—and thus our waterspeed—is 50 knots. And if we were to try to take off or land

166 Appendix C

downwind on that lake? Our waterspeed would be 60 knots + 10 knots = 70 knots!

But what if there is current, which there will be in a river or in coastal tidal areas? Now we have to adjust our groundspeed for the current to find our waterspeed: Waterspeed will be greater than groundspeed if we are moving upstream and less than groundspeed when moving downstream.

So let's imagine a river flowing north to south at 5 knots, and the wind is from the south at 10 knots. What is our waterspeed if we touch down at an airspeed of 60 knots heading 180° (i.e., downstream, or with the current, and into the wind)? Remember, waterspeed is groundspeed ± current. And groundspeed is airspeed minus headwind. So our groundspeed is 60 knots − 10 knots = 50 knots. And when going downstream (i.e., with the current), waterspeed is groundspeed minus current, which is 50 knots − 5 knots = 45 knots.

And what if we were to land to the north on that same river with the same wind? Now our groundspeed at touchdown is 60 knots + 10 knots = 70 knots, and because we're landing into the current, our waterspeed is groundspeed + current, or 70 knots + 5 knots = 75 knots. That's 30 knots more waterspeed than if we had landed to the south!

The two situations we just discussed are, it turns out, the best-case and the worst-case scenarios with respect to waterspeed for takeoff and landing:

- *Best choice* for landing and taking off: into the wind (upwind) and with the current (downstream).

- *Worst choice* for landing and taking off: downwind and against the current (upstream).

Other situations are intermediate. For example, let's say in that same river later that day the wind shifts to the north at 10 knots. If we were to take off or land heading north at an airspeed of 60 knots, groundspeed would be 60 knots − 10 knots = 50 knots, and waterspeed would be 50 knots + 5 knots = 55 knots. And if with that 10-knot north wind we were to take off or land heading south at 60

Appendix C   167

knots airspeed, our groundspeed would be 60 + 10 = 70 knots, and our waterspeed would be 70 − 5 = 65 knots.

So with a 10-knot wind and a 5-knot current, following is the order of preference with respect to waterspeed for takeoff and landing, from best case to worst case:

1. (Best case) Upwind and downstream: waterspeed 45 knots

2. Upwind and upstream: waterspeed 55 knots

3. Downwind and downstream: waterspeed 65 knots

4. (Worst case) Downwind and upstream: waterspeed 75 knots

For both taking off and landing, upwind and downstream will *always* be the best case, and downwind and upstream will *always* be the worst case for waterspeed. Other combinations will depend on the strength of the wind and the strength of the current, but if wind is greater than current, waterspeed will be lower if you take off or land into the wind; if current is greater than wind, waterspeed will be lower if you take off or land downstream. And in reality, unless the breeze is very slight, wind speed will generally be greater than current, so if in doubt, land into the wind.

One final consideration: When the direction of the wind is opposite the direction of the current, you can expect the water surface to be choppier than if the wind and current are in the same direction. So for both the best-case and worst-case scenarios for waterspeed on takeoff and landing, the water surface will be choppier than for the intermediate cases. A little chop is helpful when taking off, as it helps the floats break free from the water surface.

Idle Taxiing after Landing

Once you've landed with minimum waterspeed, you're not done dealing with current—not by a long shot. Let's say with a 10-knot wind and 5-knot current (which is a very fast current, but it makes the math easier), you've landed with the best-case combination— upwind and downstream. After landing, you have come off the step and put your water rudders down, and now you want to idle taxi to the dock. Suppose you touched down abeam the dock, and you're now downstream of the dock, so you will need to turn around to head back upstream to the dock.

Think about the effectiveness of your water rudders when you've come off the step after touchdown, before making any turn. Your groundspeed while idle taxiing may be about 5 knots, and if the current you're riding with is 5 knots, that means your waterspeed is *zero*: That is, there is no water flowing past your water rudders, so their effectiveness is nil. Therefore, any directional control you have will come from the air rudder, which is acted upon by propwash and by the headwind. What if you now try to make that 180° turn back to the dock using air rudder? As soon as you start to turn, the wind will weathervane you back to windward. Give it more throttle? No, you'll just bury the bows of the floats.

What are your options in this scenario? Sail backward to the dock? Possibly, if the wind is strong and the current is light, but otherwise the current will likely prevent you from making progress upstream, and the 10-knot wind in this scenario would be unlikely to overcome the 5-knot current. You could (at least in theory) do a plow taxi turn, which has all the drawbacks discussed in the study guide. Or you could get back on the step in the landing direction and try a step taxi turn if the river or waterway is wide enough, which it often will not be. But let's say you accomplished one of those two maneuvers to make a 180° turn, so now you're headed back upstream toward the dock. Now you're moving upstream (with a waterspeed of 5 knots + 5 knots = 10 knots), meaning your water rudders will be very effective. And in general, approaching a dock upstream (i.e., into the current) is a good thing, not only because the water rudders are effective but also because the current helps stop you as you approach the dock. But in this case you are taxiing downwind, so if the wind is not exactly on your tail, it will weathervane you back to windward. Now it's a matter of whether the good water rudder effectiveness is enough to overcome the weathervaning tendency. The stronger the wind and the lighter the current, the less likely it is that you will be able to maintain directional control as you approach the dock. (And don't forget: When idle taxiing downwind, you hold

Appendix C 169

the control wheel full *forward* (not aft) to avoid burying the bows of the floats.)

If the weathervaning tendency exceeds your ability to maintain directional control with water rudders, what else can you do? From your position downstream of the dock, you could step taxi upstream of the dock, come off the step (don't make a step taxi turn from downwind to upwind, for reasons discussed in the study guide), and when idle taxiing, both the water rudders and weathervaning will help you turn very easily back downstream toward the dock. Again, your water rudders will not be effective as you idle taxi downstream, but your air rudder will be effective in this 10-knot wind, and this may allow you enough directional control to approach the dock safely and under control. Note, though, that once you shut the engine down you will no longer have propwash over your air rudder, so directional control will decrease, and even with the engine shut down you will be approaching the dock at 5 knots due to current alone. You will have to step onto the dock quickly to stop the aircraft. (Note also that you will need to keep the floats parallel to the dock: If the sterns of the floats are allowed to drift out into the current, the current will act on the sterns of the floats to turn the aircraft around—though in this scenario the weathervaning tendency due to the wind would counteract that.)

So what should you do? In the given (very challenging) set of conditions, I would probably come off the step downstream of the dock (i.e., past it), try to make the idle taxi turn upwind to downwind, and try to taxi to the dock downwind but into the current. With 15+ knots of wind, I would try to sail to the dock. Others will no doubt have different answers.

So far, we've been considering idle taxiing following the best case for waterspeed on landing: landing into the wind and downstream. We've seen that the best case for waterspeed on landing is not the best case for idle taxiing after landing.

Now let's consider idle taxiing after touchdown with that same 10-knot wind and 5-knot current, with one of the combinations of wind and current that gives less favorable waterspeed at touchdown—landing upwind and upstream (i.e., into the wind and against the current):

170 **Appendix C**

- Ability to idle taxi in the landing direction is *ideal*—water rudder and air rudder are both very effective.

- *Landing strategy*—Come off the step downstream of the dock, and idle taxi upstream to the dock. If the current is small (1–2 knots), this may actually be your best overall choice, even though your waterspeed at touchdown is a little higher than if you had landed with the current.

You can think through the exercise of landing downwind/upstream and downwind/downstream, but in reality landing downwind is seldom going to be the best choice.

Note that all of this is dependent on the relative strength of wind and current. And while wind and current affect *waterspeed* equally (i.e., a 5-knot wind and a 5-knot current have the same effect on your waterspeed for takeoff and landing), current far outweighs wind in its effect on your speed relative to the dock you're trying to dock at. It would likely take a headwind component several times the speed of the current to hold you motionless relative to the dock if docking downstream (with the current).

I based the scenarios in the discussion preceding this paragraph on a wind of 10 knots and a (very brisk) current of 5 knots. Had the wind been 3 knots and the current 5 knots, for example, you could (and probably should) come off the step downstream of the dock. You likely would to be able to make a 180° idle taxi turn with the water rudders, and once turned upstream, the water rudders will be very effective and the weathervaning tendency from your tailwind will be slight. If on the other hand the wind were 15 knots and the current 1–2 knots, I would likely land into the wind even though I would be landing against the current, and I would come off the step downwind of the dock—i.e., before I was abeam of the dock—and idle taxi upwind to the dock, even though that would mean approaching the dock with the current. With this approach, while idle taxiing I would expect the control I'd get from the air rudder with this much headwind to outweigh the decreased effectiveness of the water rudders from taxiing with the current. While coasting to the dock after shutting the engine down, I would expect the wind to slow my forward progress relative to the dock despite the current.

Appendix C   171

Though some choices are better than others, there is often no single right answer. Make your plan based on the concepts above, and if it's not working out—for example, if you thought the effect of wind was going to outweigh the effect of current, and it turns out that it doesn't—then revise your plan accordingly.

Index

A
abort point, 64, 65, 74, 84, 86
ACS. *See* Airman Certification
  Standards (ACS)
after operating in water checklist,
  44
Airman Certification Standards
  (ACS), 105
  seaplane instructor's guide to, xiv
  tasks required for ASES
    candidates, xiii, xiv–xvi, 139,
    149–154
"Avoiding Ultimate Static Stability"
  (Hensch), 146

B
beaching, 96–97
  flight lesson, 21
  ground lesson, 14–15
before landing checklist, 159
boating
  navigation rules, 54–56
  terminology, 56–60
briefing
  passenger, 36, 65, 146
  self, 65

C
center of buoyancy (CB), 100, 127,
  166
checklists
  emergency, 45–48
  mnemonics, 155–162
  normal, 33–44
checkride
  ACS tasks on, xv–xvii, 149–154
  application for, xvii
  endorsements for, xvii
  preparing for, xvii, 139–141
climb checklist, 40
COLREGS, 54
confined area landing, 94
confined area takeoff, 72, 80–81
crosswind water landing, 88–89
crosswind water takeoff, 76–77
cruise checklist, 40, 159
current, 74, 83, 163–172

D
DeRemer, Dale, xi
descent checklist, 41
differences, seaplane vs. land plane,
  50–53

173

displacement, float, 60
docking, 97–99, 137
    checklist, 43
    checklist mnemonic, 161
    flight lesson, 21, 22
    ground lesson, 14–15
dock lines, securing, 60, 97, 98
drag, 51, 72, 75–76, 77, 83
    on floats, 164–166

E
electrical system malfunctions,
        checklists, 48
emergency
    checklists, 45–48
    descent, 136
    procedures, ground lesson, 14–15
    water landing, 95
endorsements, xvii
engine, before starting checklist, 36
engine, starting checklist, 37
engine failure checklists, 45

F
fetch, 78
flight review, 144
float inspection, 34
floatplane, 50–51
float pumping, 56, 129–130
floats
    amphib, 50
    straight, 50, 57
float terminology
    bow, 56
    bulkhead, 56, 57
    chine, 57
    deck, 56
    hull, 56
    keel, 56
    rudder, 56
    skeg, 56
    stern, 56

flying boat, 49, 50
Flying Floats video, 2
Frey, J. J., xi, 145

G
glassy water, 61, 62, 90
glassy water landing, 90–92
glassy water takeoff, 77–78
GUMPFARTS, 66

H
Hensch, Dave, 146, 155
history, seaplane, 49–50

I
IACRA (Integrated Airman
        Certification and Rating
        Application), xvii, 140
idle taxiing, 67–72, 127, 168–172
    downwind, 72
    turning while, 70
IMSAFE checklist, 33, 64
Intracoastal Waterway, 56

J
J-turn, 72

K
knot
    bowline, 59, 60
    cleat hitch, 58, 60
    taut line hitch, 59, 60
    two half hitches, 58, 60

L
landing
    after, checklists, 43–44
    before, checklists, 41–42
    checklists, 42–43, 160–161
    runway, 103–104
    water, 82–96, 126
        confined area, 94
        crosswind, 88–89
        effects of wind and current,
            163–172

flight lesson, 18–21
glassy, 90–92
ground lesson, 12
normal, 88
on amphib floats, 52–53, 86–87, 126
on straight floats, 84–85
power-off emergency, 95
preparing for, 82–83
rough, 92–93
landing area, assessing, 63–64
landing distance
amphib
on land, 31
on water, 29
estimating, 64
straight floats, 27
landing gear malfunctions, checklists, 46–48
landing gear procedures, 52–54, 82, 101, 125
landing gear warning, 86, 109
last visual reference (LVR), 90–92

M

maneuvering on the water, 67–74
flight lesson, 16
ground lesson, 11
Mees, Burke, xi, 146
mnemonics, checklists, 155–162
Multi-Engine Sea Rating, 145

N

"No Greater Burden: Surviving an Aircraft Accident" video, 53
normal water landing, 88
normal water takeoff, 75–76
flight lesson, 18
Notes of a Seaplane Instructor (Mees), xi, 146

O

oral exam preparation questions, 105–138

P

passenger briefing, 36, 65, 146
PAVE checklist, 33, 65
pitchpoling, 52, 71, 126, 166
plow taxi, 68
plow taxi turn, 68, 69, 70, 127, 132
porpoising, 71, 132
power-off emergency landing, 95
checklist, 46
practical test preparation, 139–141
preflight
checklists, 33–36
ground lesson, 10–11
inspection, 65, 129, 146
preparation, 10–11
procedures, 64–66

R

right-of-way, 54–55
rough water landing, 92–93
rough water takeoff, 78–79
rudders, water, 56
runway operations, 100–104
ground lesson, 14–15

S

SAFE briefing checklist, 65
safety, seaplane, xiii, 53, 146
sailing, seaplane, 56, 73–74, 97, 138, 169, 170
Seabird 1850/1850A, xxi, 23
checklists, 33–48
electrical system, 124–125
fuel system, 122–123
landing gear hydraulic system, 122–123
limitations, 24–25
performance, 24–31
specifications, 24–25
taxiing in, 131
Seaplane Ops Guide, 146
Seaplane Pilots Association, 53, 143, 146–147
seaplane rental, 143–144

Index 175

Seaplane Safety for 14 CFR Part 91 Operators (AC 91–69), 146
Seaplane Safety Institute, 145
"Seaplane Safety—License to Learn" video, 88
Seaplane, Skiplane, and Float/ Ski Equipped Helicopter Operations Handbook, 2
Seaplane Training Guide, 143, 147
shutdown checklist, 162
skid, 51
slip, 51
  forward, 136, 149
step taxiing, 68–73
  downwind, 72, 80
  turning while, 71
study guide, 49–104
syllabus, 2
  flight, 16–22
  ground, 6–15

T

takeoff
  before, checklists, 38, 156
  checklists, 39–40, 158
  runway
    crosswind, 102
    normal, 101
  water, 74–81
    confined area, 80–81
    crosswind, 76–77
    effects of wind and current, 163–172
    flight lesson, 18–21
    glassy, 77–78
    normal, 75–76
    rough, 78–79
takeoff distance
  amphib
    on land, 30
    on water, 28
  estimating, 64
  straight floats, 26

taxiing, 52
  center of bouyancy during, 127
  downwind, 72
  idle, 67–72, 168–172
  in crosswind, 68, 100
  on runway (amphib), 100
  plow, 68–70
  procedure checklist, 66
  step, 68–73
traffic pattern, 116
  amphib seaplane, 86–87
  straight-float seaplane, 84–85
training
  preparing for, xxi, 1–3
  syllabus, 5–22
transitioning to seaplanes, 51–54
turns
  idle taxi, 70
  J-turn, 72
  plow taxi, 70
  step taxi, 71

W

Water Flying magazine, 146, 147, 155
Water Landing Directory app, 128, 147
waterloop, 166
waterspeed, 164–171
water surface, reading, 61–62
  ripples, 61, 63, 127
  streaks, 61, 63
  whitecaps, 61
wave height, 78, 92
wavelength, 78, 92
weathervane, 51, 60, 127, 134, 170
  reverse, 100, 102, 127, 134
wind direction, 52, 60
  assessing, 63
wind, effect on takeoff and landing, 163–172
wind shadow, 63
wind speed, 61–62
  assessing, 61–62
WINGS Pilot Proficiency Program, 145

176   Index

About the Author

Bill Young is a seaplane pilot and instructor and a former owner of a Cessna 185 on amphibious floats. He holds an Airline Transport Pilot Certificate and Commercial Airplane Single-Engine Sea and Multi-Engine Sea Ratings. He is a Cessna Citation XL/XLS charter pilot and is a CFII, with 3,000 hours of flying time. He also holds Instrument Ground Instructor and Advanced Ground Instructor Certificates.

This book is adapted from the manual he wrote for his own students in the Cessna 185 amphib. He hopes it will help you become a proficient and safe seaplane pilot, and that a foundation of proficiency and safety will free you to appreciate the beauty and fun of flying floats.

Bill is a retired pediatric ophthalmologist. He and his wife, Barbara, are parents of three adult children and live with two Corgis in Greensboro, North Carolina, and Johns Island, South Carolina.